COMPARING TEXTS

'A brilliant series – an absolute gift for the teachers! This superb series makes clear tangible terminology and implicit meanings which to many students seem foreign. The books' methods and tactics are enjoyable and workable for both students and teachers, and the clear, evaluative and reflective models will enable students to obtain the necessary reflection in their own written responses.'

Kesner Ridge, Hagley Roman Catholic High School, Worcestershire, and Outstanding New Teacher 2002 (*The Guardian Teaching Awards*)

'This is the series we've all been waiting for! Tightly focused on the assessment objectives, these books provide an excellent aid to classroom teaching and self-study. Whether your school changes board or text, or decides to offer Literature and/or Language to 6th formers these books are still the tool that can make a real difference to results.'

Emmeline McChleery, Aylesford School, Warwick

Routledge A Level English Guides equip AS and A2 Level students with the skills they need to explore, evaluate and enjoy English. What has – until now – been lacking for the revised English A Levels is a set of text books that equip students with the concepts, skills and knowledge they need to succeed in light of the way the exams are actually working. The *Routledge A Level English Guides* series fills this critical gap.

Books in the series are built around the various skills specified in the assessment objectives (AOs) for all AS and A2 Level English courses, and take into account how these AOs are being interpreted by the exam boards. Focusing on the AOs most relevant to their topic, the books help students to develop their knowledge and abilities through analysis of lively texts and contemporary data. Each book in the series covers a different area of language and literary study, and offers accessible **explanations**, **examples**, **exercises**, **summaries**, **suggested answers** and a **glossary of key terms**.

The series helps students to learn what is required of them and develop skills accordingly, while ensuring that English remains an exciting subject that students enjoy studying. The books are also an essential resource for teachers trying to create lessons that balance the demands of the exam boards with the more general skills and knowledge students need for the critical appreciation of English Language and Literature.

ROUTLEDGE A LEVEL ENGLISH GUIDES

About the Series Editor

Adrian Beard was Head of English at Gosforth High School, Newcastle upon Tyne. He now works at the University of Newcastle Upon Tyne and is a Chief Examiner for AS and A2 Level English Literature. He is co-series editor of the Routledge Intertext series, and his publications include *Texts and Contexts*, *The Language of Politics* and *The Language of Sport* (all for Routledge).

TITLES IN THE SERIES

The Language of Literature
Adrian Beard

How Texts Work
Adrian Beard

Language and Social Contexts
Amanda Coultas

Writing for Assessment
Angela Goddard

Original Writing
Sue Morkane

Transforming Texts
Shaun O'Toole

Texts through History
Adele Wills

COMPARING TEXTS

Nicola Onyett

Routledge
Taylor & Francis Group

LONDON AND NEW YORK

First published 2005
by Routledge
2 Park Square, Milton Park, Abingdon, Oxon OX14 4RN

Simultaneously published in the USA and Canada
by Routledge
270 Madison Ave, New York, NY 10016

Routledge is an imprint of the Taylor & Francis Group

Typeset in Galliard by Keystroke, Jacaranda Lodge, Wolverhampton
Printed and bound in Great Britain by TJ International Ltd,
Padstow, Cornwall

British Library Cataloguing in Publication Data
A catalogue record for this book is available from the British Library

Library of Congress Cataloging in Publication Data
Onyett, Nicola, 1966–
   Comparing texts / Nicola Onyett.
      p. cm. — (Routledge A level English guides)
   1. English literature—Explication—Examinations—Study guides.
2. English literature—Examinations—Study guides. I. Title. II. Series.
   PR21.O595 2005
   807′.6—dc22

                                                2004009295

ISBN 0–415–32859–4 (pbk)

CONTENTS

PREFACE

This book explores the relationships that exist between texts. It focuses on skills and concepts rather than particular texts, and centres on how you might approach comparing the sort of literary and non-literary texts that you will encounter as you study AS/A2 English. As readers, we can spend so much of our time looking for what is original about a writer's approach that we can overlook the fact that all texts are written, received and understood within a network of other texts. When we read new text we apply what we already know about how texts work to construct meanings as we read. The book looks at how comparing texts can cast fresh light upon them.

Each chapter of this book contains several exercises. When the exercise introduces a new idea, there will usually be suggestions for answer immediately following. When the exercise is testing to see if an idea has been fully understood, suggestions for answer are given at the back of the book on page 71. Research-based exercises do not have suggestions for answer, and some tasks are designed to stimulate ideas or encourage classroom discussion, and stand alone because suggested answers might narrow down your range of potential answers. Technical terms, defined in the Glossary on page 77, are printed in bold when used for the first time.

ASSESSMENT OBJECTIVES

AS and A2 examination specifications are underpinned by core Assessment Objectives (AOs), which set out the knowledge and skills you need to acquire during the course. The key AOs addressed in this book are as follows:

English Literature

A01: in writing about literary texts, you must use appropriate terminology

A02: you must show knowledge and understanding of literary texts of different types and periods, exploring and commenting on relationships and comparisons between literary texts

A03: you must show how writers' choices of form, structure and language shape meanings

A04: you must provide independent opinions and judgements, informed by different interpretations of literary texts by other readers

A05: you must look at contextual factors which affect the way texts are written, read and understood

English Language and Literature

A01: you must show knowledge and understanding of texts gained from the combined study of literary and non-literary texts

A02: in responding to literary and non-literary texts, you must distinguish, describe and interpret variation in meaning and form

A03: you must respond to and analyse texts, using literary and linguistic concepts and approaches

A04: you must show understanding of the ways contextual variation and choices of form, style and vocabulary shape the meanings of texts

English Language

A01: in writing about texts, you must use appropriate terminology

A03: you must show a systematic approach to analysing texts

A05: you must analyse the ways contextual factors affect the way texts are written, read and understood

Beyond the Assessment Objectives, however, setting texts beside each other rather than studying them in isolation enables us to tap into the wider question of how we as readers make judgements about anything. It is much easier to discuss a text if you have a reference point to check it against. Comparing texts makes us look at the ideas that emerge from the gaps between them. Rather than taking a text for granted, if we link it to others we can challenge it more critically, assessing both what it is and what it is not. We are unlikely to become passive readers who lose sight of the writing process (and the infinite variety of approaches writers can take) if we have a framework for investigating similarities and differences between texts. This book presents a range of strategies, techniques and perspectives to help you compare texts effectively.

ACKNOWLEDGEMENTS

I would like to thank the following people for their contributions during the writing of this book: Robert, Lydia and Madeleine Onyett; Alan Shutt; Rosalind Moad; Adrian Beard, Christabel Kirkpatrick and Kate Parker (editorial help, advice and support); Ruth Doyle, Ian Giles, Jill Fairley and Julia Millhouse (ideas, encouragement and a regular supply of chocolate) and, of course, the many past and present A Level Language and Literature students at Queen Margaret's School, York without whom *Comparing Texts* would never have been written.

The author would like to thank the following copyright holders for permission to reproduce material in this book:

Extract from *South Wind through the Kitchen* by Elizabeth David, originally published in *Summer Cooking* (1955). Used by permission of Jill Norman, literary trustee, on behalf of the estate of Elizabeth David.

Extract from *How to Be a Domestic Goddess* by Nigella Lawson, published by Chatto & Windus (2000). Used by permission of The Random House Group Limited.

Extract from *Heartburn* by Nora Ephron. Reprinted by permission of International Creative Management, Inc. Copyright © 1985 by Nora Ephron.

Extract from 'Look Black in Anger' by Ben Marshall (2002). Used by permission of *The Guardian*.

'Anne Hathaway' from *The World's Wife* by Carol Ann Duffy. Copyright © 1999 by Carol Ann Duffy. Reprinted in North America by permission of Faber and Faber, an affiliate of Farrar, Straus and Giroux, LLC and by permission of Macmillan Ltd in the rest of the world.

GENRE

CHAPTER 1

This chapter focuses on the impact and importance of **genre** upon the way we read and receive texts. A genre is the framework within which a particular type of text operates – the rules of the game, if you like. The oldest established use of the term 'genre' refers to the classical literary text types of poetry, prose and drama, and these neat categories are often used to organise and shape the way we respond to certain texts and create our own meanings. Our expectations of each new text we come across are based upon either our previous experience of similar texts, or the way in which a new text is presented. This network of links between texts is called **intertextuality**. If you read a sequel to a novel you have enjoyed, you would expect it to relate to the first text in some way, perhaps by picking up where the previous narrative had left off, or by following the same characters through another series of adventures. If you read a detective novel, you take it for granted that narrative closure will involve the solution to the central crime of the story – which is why thrillers are often known as 'whodunits'. Moreover, if your English teacher tells you that you that you will be studying a particular novel as an examination text, you might reasonably expect it to be a famous work by a great writer. Most A Level students would be surprised to be presented with a copy of *The Tale of the Flopsy Bunnies*.

TEXT CONVENTIONS

If you think about the advertising and marketing of books, television programmes and films, you will see how the producers of these media texts rely on the audience's knowledge of generic conventions. Next time you are in a bookshop, notice how, for instance, romantic novels aimed at young women (often referred to as 'chick-lit') are grouped together and identified by their bright pastel front covers and modern cartoon illustrations. J.K. Rowling's Harry Potter books are sold in bright jackets with vivid illustrations and similar typeface for children, but with redesigned, black-and-white, graphic front covers for adults. Television soap operas, with their regular characters and continuous action, are designed to catch the early evening audiences that the programme schedulers hope will stay tuned to a particular channel for the rest of the evening. The soaps are closely identified with their channels and function as brand identifiers: *EastEnders* denotes BBC1, *Coronation Street* ITV1 and *Hollyoaks* Channel 4.

Next time you go to the cinema, see how film trailers try to hook you by linking a new release to a previous success. This is one of the key reasons for the success of franchise films such as the *Scream* series; the audience that pays to see *Scream III* has a good working knowledge of the generic conventions of not only horror movies in general, but the horror-spoof **subgenre** in particular. The way in which we receive and understand media texts shapes and controls our expectations of them. Generic practices and conventions provide us with a yardstick against which to measure our responses; they tell us how to think about texts.

In order to understand how texts work, we need to familiarise ourselves with their machinery. Both writers and readers are aware of generic conventions, and much of the interest which emerges as we extract our own meanings from a particular text is located in the extent to which we are aware of the writer's ideas and intentions.

Exercise 1 – Omelette à l'Oseille

Read the following complete text and place it within the genre that seems most appropriate to you. Suggestions for answer follow.

Elizabeth David

Omelette à l'Oseille (1955)

One of the nicest of summer omelettes. Wash a handful of sorrel; chop it. Melt it in butter; add salt. In five minutes it is ready to add to the eggs.

Suggestions for Answer

This text follows the classical recipe format, describing how to prepare a simple meal. The reader deduces that the French title (French being the traditional language of fine cooking) means 'sorrel omelette' because of the ingredients listed. Elizabeth David begins with an authoritative pronouncement on the dish, but does not describe its flavour in any detail. Her voice is cool, concise and economical; her sophisticated punctuation, particularly the use of semi-colons, enables her to compress a lot of information into brief but weighty sentences.

CASE STUDY: THE RECIPE GENRE

This text contains ideas and information about food preparation. Like all the other extracts in this chapter it can be categorised as a recipe, and this generic similarity is a useful perspective from which to compare the form, structure and language of the following texts.

Exercise 2 – Key Lime Pie

Read the following text from *How to Be a Domestic Goddess* and list the linguistic elements that support a recipe classification. Suggestions for answer are at the back of the book.

Nigella Lawson (2000)

What follows are two versions of key lime pie, although there is little chance of using fresh key limes. You can use bottled key lime juice (or so it's claimed), but I tend to use ordinary limes.

A note on crusts: it's traditional to use digestive biscuits, but I wanted to make a chocolate-based one as well, I suppose in memory of the chocolate lime sweets I ate as a child. If you use chocolate digestives, it's hard to cut the tart once it's been fridged so I suggest you use ordinary digestives with a tea-spoonful of cocoa added when you mix them with the butter. Ginger nuts work very well, too: and I love using coconut biscuits.

And as far as the filling goes, don't expect a lime pie to be green. It's yellow – though the first pie is slightly greener because of the zest. A really green pie is a dyed pie.

The following seems to be the basic model for a key lime pie: and it's the one in Jane Grigson's monumentally absorbing *Fruit Book*. Don't be put off by the idea of condensed milk. It's essential and the sourness of the limes totally sees off its temple-aching sugariness.

For the base:	For the filling:
200g digestive biscuits	5 large egg yolks
50g softened, unsalted butter	397g can sweetened condensed milk
Springform tin	zest of 3 limes
	150ml lime juice (of 4–5 limes)
	3 large egg whites

Preheat the over to 160°C/gas mark 3 and put in a baking sheet.

Put the biscuits and butter into the processor and blitz till all's reduced to oily crumbs. Press these into the tin, lining the bottom and going a little way up the sides, and chill in the fridge while you get on with the rest.

You will need an electric mixer to do this. I always use my KitchenAid, but a hand-held one is fine. Beat the egg yolks until thick, add the can of condensed milk, grated zest and the lime juice. Whisk the egg whites separately until soft peaks form, then fold gently into the yolk mixture. Pour into the lined tin and cook for 25 minutes, when the filling should be firm. It may puff up and then, on cooling, fall, but that's the deal.

Leave to cool on a rack before unmoulding, and chill well.

Serves 6–8.

Suggestions for Answer

Your response to this exercise represents your working knowledge of how the recipe genre operates. You have identified a series of patterns and structures within this text, which you associate with the recipe genre; however, you may also have processed additional information. Because Nigella Lawson is a well-known food writer, you would not expect her to be writing a novel, poem or comedy sketch: your pre-existing knowledge and understanding has therefore shaped your expectations of this new text.

The primary function of a recipe is to instruct the reader and many of the discourse features of this extract underpin that purpose. Yet aspects of the text do not square with a recipe categorisation. These awkwardnesses should make you think about our tendency as readers to pigeonhole texts, and the constraints of too narrow a classification. Most writing is multi-functional, working on several levels at once rather than sticking slavishly to a single theme or purpose.

The **register** of this text indicates that it is aimed at a well-educated audience with a wide vocabulary and an interest in the work of other experts. An academic style is created as Lawson cites a related reference text for potential further reading, Jane Grigson's *Fruit Book*. A noticeable feature of her prose is the lavish use of personalised description, such as the unusual choice of the verb 'fridged', rather than 'chilled', and the vivid physical accuracy of the noun phrase 'temple-aching sugariness' for an oversweet taste. The punctuation is often complex and unusual: the effect of three carefully placed commas followed by a colloquial punch line adds interest to the sentence, 'It may puff up and then, on cooling, fall, but that's the deal.' This decorative and embellished style is more complex and idiosyncratic than we might expect of a straightforward set of instructions.

How to Be a Domestic Goddess was accompanied by a Channel 4 television series. It is, in a sense, a written version of a performance text received visually by the viewers. The written form must, therefore, convey something of the author's personality to recreate the relationship between Lawson as seen on television and her viewers at home, and this overrides the impersonal instructional conventions of the recipe genre. Moreover, not everyone who reads this text intends to make the pie; many readers will have bought *How to Be a Domestic Goddess* to make a statement about their own actual or fantasy lifestyle, rather than as an instruction manual. Marketing and publicity present Lawson's books as a way to recreate the glamorous and aspirational existence her audience has seen on television.

Exercise 3 – The Domestic Goddess

Analyse the following extract, also from Nigella Lawson's *How to Be a Domestic Goddess*, noting

(a) any discourse features that confirm that it is still within the recipe genre and
(b) those that challenge this categorisation.

Suggestions for answer follow on page 6.

This is a book about baking, but not a baking book – not in the sense of being a manual or a comprehensive guide or a map of a land you do not inhabit. I neither want to confine you to kitchen quarters nor even suggest that it might be desirable. But I do think that many of us have become alienated from the domestic sphere, and that it can actually make us feel better to claim back some of that space, make it comforting rather than frightening. In a way, baking stands both as a useful metaphor for the familial warmth of the kitchen we fondly imagine used to exist, and as a way of reclaiming our lost Eden. This is hardly a culinary matter, of course: but cooking, we know, has a way of cutting through things, and to things, which have nothing to do with the kitchen. This is why it matters.

The trouble with much modern cooking is not that the food it produces isn't good, but that the mood it induces in the cook is one of the skin-of-the-teeth efficiency, all briskness and little pleasure. Sometimes that's the best we can manage, but at other times we don't want to feel like a post-modern, post-feminist, overstretched woman but, rather a domestic goddess, trailing nutmeggy fumes of baking pie in our languorous wake.

So what I'm talking about is not *being* a domestic goddess exactly, but *feeling* like one. One of the reasons making cakes is satisfying is that the effort required is so much less than the gratitude conferred. Everyone seems to think it's hard to make a cake (and no need to disillusion them), but it doesn't take more than 25 minutes to make and bake a tray of muffins or a sponge layer cake, and the returns are high: you feel disproportionately good about yourself afterwards. That is what baking, what all of this book, is about: feeling good, wafting along in the warm, sweet-smelling air, unwinding, no longer being entirely being an office creature; and that's exactly what I mean by 'comfort cooking'.

Part of it too is about a fond, if ironic, dream: the unexpressed 'I' that is a cross between Sophia Loren and Debbie Reynolds in pink cashmere cardigan and fetching gingham pinny, a weekend alter-ego winning adoring glances and endless approbation from anyone who has the good fortune to eat in her kitchen. The good thing is, we don't have to get ourselves up in Little Lady drag and we don't have to renounce the world and enter into a life of domestic drudgery. But we can bake a little – and a cake is just a cake, far easier than getting the timing right for even the most artlessly casual of midweek dinner parties.

This isn't a dream; what's more, it isn't even a nightmare.

Suggestions for Answer

This text (the preface to *How to Be a Domestic Goddess*) differs from Nigella Lawson's key lime pie recipe in being theoretical rather than practical. The **narrative structure** of **polemic** is used and the text is an essay set out in paragraphs. Baking is presented as an act of profound cultural significance. The first sentence presents the reader with a **paradox** that undermines the main purpose of a cookery book at a stroke, by denying that this text will tell you how to bake. Lawson states that she is using cookery as a metaphor for the role of modern women; it is not the practicality of baking that matters, but the psychology and sociology of it. She polarises the modern career woman who is too busy to cook for pleasure and the 1950s 'domestic goddess, trailing nutmeggy fumes of baking pie in her wake', using **hyperbole** to add an **ironic**, humorous feel; baking is presented as 'a way of reclaiming our lost Eden'.

Her deviation from the traditional recipe form is clear from the verbs she uses. Rather than the imperative form associated with the genre – mix, stir, grate, beat – Lawson uses evocative phrases such as 'feeling good', 'wafting along', 'unwinding' and 'winning adoring glances'. Again, unlike the conventional impersonal and context-free language of instructional writing, Lawson sets up a personal relationship with her readers, visually encoding a shared secret within the text by using parentheses: 'Everyone seems to think it's hard to bake a cake (and no need to disillusion them) . . . '. This trick creates an exclusive team us-and-them feel. She concludes with a forceful, single-sentence paragraph that acts as a punchline, encapsulating the argument and providing a final intriguing thought: 'this isn't a dream; what's more, it isn't even a nightmare'.

Lawson's **allusions** overstep the conventional boundaries of the recipe genre by referring to the Bible, post-modernism, post-feminism and iconic Hollywood stars of the 1950s. This wide frame of reference shows that the preface is a recipe text in only a limited sense. Lawson's ironic, conspiratorial humour refocuses the text, presenting baking not as a skill or craft to be taught or explained, but rather as a nostalgic (almost comic) hobby for professional women who can laugh at the idea of swapping their power suits for a 'pink cashmere cardigan and fetching gingham pinny'. This creation of an alternative reality makes it necessary to reclassify this text. Perhaps you can think of a suitable label for a revised category or subgenre within which it might operate: is it fantasy cookery? Food fiction?

Exercise 4 – Key Lime Pie Again

Read the following extract from the semi-autobiographical novel *Heartburn*. The narrator, Delia, is a New York cookery writer whose husband, Mark, is having an affair with another woman, Thelma. Analyse the style and voice of this text, picking out discourse features not normally associated with the recipe genre. Suggestions for answer follow the text.

Nora Ephron (1985)

If I had to do it over again, I would have made a different kind of pie. The pie I threw at Mark made a terrific mess but a blueberry pie would have been even better, since it would have permanently ruined his new blazer, the one we bought with Thelma. But Betty said bring a Key lime pie, so I did. The Key lime pie is very simple to make. First you line a 9-inch pie plate with a graham cracker crust. Then beat 6 egg yolks. Add 1 cup lime juice (even bottled lime juice will do), two 14-ounce cans sweetened condensed milk, and 1 tablespoon grated lime rind. Pour into the pie shell and freeze. Remove from freezer and spread with whipped cream. Let sit five minutes before serving.

I realise now that I should have thrown the pie (or at least done the thinking that led to the throwing of the pie) several weeks earlier than I did, but it's very hard to throw a pie at anyone when you're pregnant, because you feel so vulnerable. Also, let's face it, I wasn't ready to throw the pie. I should also add that the pie was hardly the first thing I'd thought of throwing at Mark, but every other time I'd wanted to throw something at him, I couldn't bring myself to do it. Once, for example, right after I found out about him and Thelma, I'd been seized by a violent impulse, but the only thing I could see to throw at the time was a signed Thonet chair, and I am far too bourgeois to throw a signed Thonet anything at anyone. Some time later, especially while I was in the hospital, I gave considerable thought to smashing Mark's head in with a very good frying pan I had bought at the Bridge kitchenware company, but I always knew I would never do anything of the sort, and in any case, smashing your husband's head in with a frying pan seems slightly too fraught with feminist content, if you know what I mean.

(Even now, I wonder if I would have thrown the pie had we been eating in Betty's dining room. Probably not. On the floor in Betty's dining room is a beautiful Oriental rug, and I would have been far too concerned about staining it. Fortunately, though, we were eating in the kitchen and the kitchen has a linoleum floor. That's how bourgeois I am: at the split second I picked up the pie to throw at Mark, at the split second I was about to do the bravest – albeit the most derivative – thing I had ever done in my life, I thought to myself: Thank God the floor is linoleum and can be wiped up.)

Suggestions for Answer

This text tests the viability of the recipe genre. The title *Heartburn* hints at a dual purpose: the text is about food (which can give you indigestion or heartburn), but it is also about the breakdown of a marriage (which can give you heartburn of a metaphorical sort). While Nigella Lawson blurs genre boundaries by incorporating aspects of autobiography, Nora Ephron blends a key lime pie recipe into the story of her fictional **alter ego**'s disintegrating marriage. In a conventional cookery book, the writer might warn the reader of potential problems with equipment or ingredients, but the criterion for success is the flavour of the food. In *Heartburn*, however, the pie is a failure not because it does not taste good, but because it is not a very effective assault weapon. The narrator declares that key lime pie 'is very simple to make' and should produce good results every time. But the text focuses on a specific occasion when the pie failed; the reader is told in an agitated and defensive manner of the unforeseen drawbacks of the filling. Ephron uses the pie as a comically inappropriate **conceit** that symbolises the public collapse of Delia's marriage. Inappropriate, random, scattered detail (Thonet chairs, the Bridge kitchenware company, Oriental rugs, linoleum floors) interrupt the story of the disastrous dinner party and correlate to the much larger-scale fractured narrative of Delia's life. Therefore much of the text is non-chronological, involving both narrative flashbacks and projections. This would be extremely confusing in a conventional recipe.

Above all, the tone of the piece is personal and emotional, rather than impersonal and instructional; Ephron condenses the ingredients, equipment and method into just six lines to emphasise the tragicomic insignificance of key lime pie in a crisis. In short, although the typical lexical field of food preparation is there, together with a brief section of sequential writing designed to instruct, the primary function of this text is something else altogether.

Exercise 5 – Bourdain's Butter and Garlic

Read the following extract from *Kitchen Confidential*, Anthony Bourdain's account of life as a New York chef. Compare it with the other recipe texts in this chapter, noting the discourse features that seem to

- Link this text with the others (similarities)
- Distinguish it from them (differences)

Suggestions for answers are at the back of the book.

Anthony Bourdain (2001)

In a professional kitchen, [butter is] almost always the first and last thing in the pan. We sauté in a mixture of butter and oil for the nice brown, caramelized color, and we finish nearly every sauce with it (we call this *monter au beurre*); that's why my sauce tastes richer and creamier and mellower than yours, why it's got that nice, thick, opaque consistency. Believe me, there's a big crock of softened butter on almost every cook's station, and it's getting a heavy workout. Margarine? That's not food. I Can't Believe It's Not Butter? I can. If you're planning on using margarine in *anything*, you can stop reading now, because I won't be able to help you. Even the Italians – you know, those crafty Tuscans – spout off about getting away from butter, and extol the glories of olive oil (and it *is* glorious), but pay a surprise visit to the kitchen of that three-star Northern Italian, and what's that they're sneaking into the pasta? And the risotto? The veal chop? Could it be? Is it . . . why, I can't believe it IS butter!!

Roasted garlic. Garlic is divine. Few food items can taste so many distinct ways, handled correctly. Misuse of garlic is a crime. Old garlic, burnt garlic, garlic cut too long ago, garlic that has been tragically smashed through one of those abominations, the garlic press, are all disgusting. Please treat your garlic with respect. Sliver it for pasta, like you saw in *Goodfellas*, don't burn it. Smash it, with the flat of your knife blade if you like, but *don't* put it through a press. I don't know what that junk is that squeezes out of the end of those things, but it ain't garlic. And try roasting garlic. It gets mellow and sweeter if you roast it whole, still on the clove, to be squeezed out later when it's soft and brown. Try a Caesar dressing, for instance, with a mix of fresh, raw garlic for bite, and roasted for background, and you'll see what I mean. Nothing will permeate your food more irrevocably and irreparably than burnt or rancid garlic. Avoid at all costs that vile spew you see rotting in oil in screwtop jars. Too lazy to peel fresh? You don't deserve to eat garlic.

This authorial voice sounds like one of the tough-talking Italian gangsters of Martin Scorsese's violent Mafia epic *Goodfellas*, an iconic film text with which Bourdain assumes his readers are familiar. This assumption tells the reader a good deal about the social and cultural contexts of the text, echoing and reinforcing Bourdain's aggressive 'extreme food' style. His use of the classic rhetorical **rule of three** – 'my sauce tastes richer and creamier and mellower than yours' – emphasises his effortless superiority, and this effect is extended by repeating the conjunction 'and' rather than simply using commas. Far from attempting to charm and/or reassure the reader, Bourdain is belligerent, confrontational and competitive; he expresses the world-weary, long-suffering resignation of a professional forced to condescend to amateurs. What saves the text from alienating the reader is (paradoxically) the comically exaggerated abuse he hurls at the hapless novice who will use 'tragically smashed' fresh garlic, or, even worse, jars of 'vile spew'. The implication is that Bourdain cares enough about good food and his readers to issue these dire warnings; this text may appeal to the reader's masochistic streak.

Exercise 6 – Fast Food Nation: French Fries

Read this extract describing the author's visit to a factory in Idaho, USA, which produces french fries for the McDonald's burger chain. Examine the language used to present the food production process. Suggestions for answer follow on page 10.

Eric Schlosser (2002)

Conveyor belts took the wet, clean potatoes into a machine that blasted them with steam for twelve seconds, boiled the water under their skins, and exploded their skins off. Then the potatoes were pumped into a preheated tank and shot through a Lamb Water Gun Knife. They emerged as shoestring fries. Four video cameras scrutinized them from different angles, looking for flaws. When a french fry with a blemish was detected, an optical sorting machine time-sequenced a single burst of compressed air that knocked the bad fry off the production line onto a separate conveyor belt, which carried it to a machine with tiny automatic knives that precisely removed the blemish. And then the fry was returned to the main production line.

Sprays of hot water blanched the fries, gusts of hot air dried them, and 25,000 pounds of boiling oil fried them to a slight crisp. . . . The fries were sealed in brown bags, then the bags were loaded by robots into cardboard boxes, and the boxes were stacked by robots onto wooden pallets. Forklifts driven by human beings took the pallets to a freezer for storage. Inside that freezer I saw 20 million pounds of french fries, most of them destined for McDonalds's, the boxes of fries stacked thirty feet high, the stacks extending for roughly forty yards. . . .

Near the freezer was a laboratory where women in white coats analyzed french fries day and night, measuring their sugar content, their starch content, their color. During the fall, Lamb Weston added sugar to the fries; in the spring it leached sugar out of them; the goal was to maintain a uniform taste and appearance throughout the year. Every half hour, a new batch of fries was cooked in fryers identical to those used in fast food kitchens. A middle-aged woman in a lab coat handed me a paper plate full of premium extra longs, the type of french fries sold at McDonalds's, and a salt shaker and some ketchup. The fries on the plate looked wildly out of place in this laboratory setting, this surreal food factory with its computer screens, digital readouts, shiny steel platforms, and evacuation plans in case of ammonia gas leaks. The french fries were delicious – crisp and golden brown, made from potatoes that had been in the ground that morning. I finished them and asked for more.

Suggestions for Answer

Eric Schlosser's description of the french fry production process is exact. His chronological recount is meticulous, right down to the twelve seconds it takes to remove the potato skins, and he praises the final product – 'delicious – crisp and golden brown'. However, this is an eyewitness report of an industrial process that no one could replicate in their own kitchen, and the text alienates the reader by emphasising the huge gulf between the fast food process and the way ordinary people cook for their families. Schlosser's verbs create an atmosphere of extreme violence – 'blasted', 'boiled', 'exploded', 'pumped into' and 'shot through'– while the 'video cameras', 'robots' and 'automated knives' evoke unsettling images of a futuristic potato death camp. Human beings are marginalised and depersonalised, and the chilly voice of the author breaks the link between the cook, the food and the people who will eventually eat it. The emotional and psychological side of preparing good food for the people we love – a common theme in all the other extracts in this chapter – is edited out of the text. Instead, Schlosser repulses rather than entices his readers; while still working within the parameters of the recipe genre, he subverts the traditional purpose of the text. The ultimate irony, however, is that he admits that the fries taste great even after he has witnessed the repellent production process: 'I finished them and asked for more.' While this admission seems to undermine his argument, in fact it emphasises the power of our uneasy addiction to junk food, and this (as *Fast Food Nation*'s subtitle *What the All-American Meal is Doing to the World* suggests) is Schlosser's central thesis.

Exercise 7 – Comparing Food Production Texts

Compare the language, form and structure and/or the audience, purpose and genre of the texts in this chapter. There are no suggestions for answer for this exercise.

CONCLUSION

This chapter has explored some ways in which the concept of genre or text types can provide a comparative framework. The exercises you have done should have reminded you of how much you already know about how texts work as well as giving you a fuller understanding of the requirements and practices of certain texts.

As an active reader, you will have begun to locate a range of interesting questions which lurk in the gaps between the texts in this chapter and the archetypal recipe genre. The recipe label still seems appropriate when the author's primary purpose is instructional, but the voices in these texts contain elements of the polemical, the political, the poetic and the romantic. In the end, you may feel that some of the texts break so many of the established and expected conventions of the genre that they barely qualify as recipes at all. This may seem a rather unsettling notion – when is a genre not a genre? – but it is just at textual stress points like these, when generic boundaries come under intense pressure, that the process of comparing texts becomes most interesting. A genre comparison is not simply a matter of attaching neat labels, but of seeing how writers can still be original while conforming to traditional practices and conventions.

Readers, writers, publishers and booksellers cross-reference and index new texts against established ones. You, as the reader, will have definite expectations of how *Comparing Texts* should work based on your understanding of how textbooks operate and I, as the writer of a book in a linked series, work from a very similar standpoint. In other words, we have a mutual vested interest in establishing very clear parameters for the textbook genre.

SUMMARY

This chapter has done the following:

- Examined notions of genre and subgenre with reference to various recipe texts
- Looked at some ideas about intertextuality and the ways in which we receive 'new' texts
- Identified ways in which ideas about genre can affect how texts are received
- Thought about the notion of a contract between writers and readers
- Looked at how generic boundaries can be blurred rather than clear-cut
- Explored ideas about how notions of genre are created in the first place

THEME

CHAPTER 2

This chapter discusses linking texts thematically. To begin with, we need a reason to compare texts – random selection may be exciting, but it is unlikely to be either productive or straightforward. We need to consider practical aspects of potential pairings or groupings of texts. In English Literature exams, texts are usually juxtaposed because they deal with aspects of the same theme. Examiners construct these thematic pairings so students can link texts purposefully and show what they know. The very least this tells you is that two writers have thought about the same subject and felt it was worth discussing.

BRIDGING THE GAP BETWEEN TEXTS

Studying different treatments of a particular theme will help you to investigate both writers' approaches and perspectives. The shared topic will lead you into a more detailed comparison of the texts, based on the similarities and differences of language, form and structure, readings and interpretations, and various contextual factors. It is important to realise that a thematic link is a means to an end – a way into your exploration of these areas, rather than the primary focus of your writing.

Thematic comparisons can be trickier than they seem. Focusing solely upon the similarities between texts can be a rather sterile exercise; it is often more useful to probe the differences between them than to list links that may be marginal on the one hand, or obvious on the other. The first thing to consider is the topic itself. The best subject to choose (if it is you, and not your teacher or the examination board making the choice) is one that sparks your curiosity; the organising principle behind the best comparative studies is always 'I'm interested in this'. You will find a list of themes that have produced interesting and unusual investigations at the end of this chapter. These are not to be taken as recommended titles, but as starting points for your own ideas.

CASE STUDY: SINGLE PARENTS AND THEIR CHILDREN

One of the most popular literary subjects is that of family relationships – probably because we all have families, and our relationships with them are often complicated. In order to narrow down this vast topic, the texts in this chapter all focus on one specific aspect of family life: people who live outside the traditional pattern of a married mother and father living with their children. Over the last few centuries, many commentators have expressed strong views about single parents and their children, ranging from the relaxed and sympathetic to the condemnatory and even violent. Shifting social attitudes have had a major impact upon the words used to describe single parents and their children: The National Council for the Unmarried Mother and Her Child has been renamed The National Council for One-Parent Families, and the term 'illegitimate' is now almost as politically incorrect as the old-fashioned word 'bastard'. Yet even today, when one-parent families are common, some political, religious and media commentators still characterise lone parents as ignorant and irresponsible. Given these unfixed and shifting points of view, a comparison of texts based on this topic has potential. When there is disagreement and uncertainty surrounding a theme, we can often draw out interesting similarities and differences between texts.

Exercise 1 – Comparing Themed Texts

Read the following extracts and consider the different ways in which they present their ideas about single parents and/or their children.

Suggestions for answer follow on page 18.

Text A is an extract from J.K. Rowling's foreword to a short story collection sold to raise money for the National Council for One-Parent Families, published in 2002.

Text A

Poverty, as I soon found out, is a lot like childbirth – you know it's going to hurt before it happens, but you'll never know how much until you've experienced it. Some of the newspaper articles written about me have come close to romanticising the time I spent on Income Support, because the well-worn cliché of the writer starving in the garret is so much more picturesque than the bitter reality of living in poverty with a child.

The endless little humiliations of life on benefits – and let us remember that six out of ten families headed by a lone parent live in poverty – receive very little media coverage unless they are followed by what seems to be, in newsprint at least, a swift and Cinderella-like reversal of fortune. I remember reaching the checkout, counting out the money in coppers, finding out that I

---

was two pence short of a tin of beans and feeling I had to pretend I had mislaid a ten pound note for the benefit of the bored girl at the till. Similarly unappreciated acting skills were required for my forays into Mothercare, where I would pretend to be examining clothes I could not afford for my daughter, while edging ever closer to the baby-changing room, where they offered a small supply of free nappies. I hated dressing my longed-for child from charity shops, I hated relying on the kindness of the relatives when it came to her new shoes; I tried furiously hard not to feel jealous of other children's beautifully decorated, well-stocked bedrooms when we went to friends' houses to play.

Text B is an extract from an historical research text called *The Family, Sex and Marriage in England, 1500–1800*, first published in 1979.

Text B

Deliberate infanticide – to become 'the butcher of her own bowels' – was a solution adopted by only the most desperate of pregnant mothers, and abandonment, both of the illegitimate and of legitimate children, was infinitely more common. As Jonas Hanway observed in 1776, 'it is much less difficult to the human heart and the dictates of self-preservation to drop a child than to kill it'. During the eighteenth century rapidly increasing numbers of infants were simply abandoned in the streets, and left to become a charge on the parish. Most of them were sent off to the parish workhouses, which were built after 1722, and where the death rate was almost as high as if they had been left in the streets. . . .

For the few who survived, the prospect was a grim one. The older females were often handed over to 'a master who is either vicious or cruel: in the one case they fall victim to his irregular passions; and in the other are subjected, with unreasonable severity, to tasks too hard to be performed.' These were the lucky ones, others being virtually enslaved by criminals and trained for a life of prostitution if female or of robbery and pick-pocketing if male. Some had their teeth torn out to serve as artificial teeth for the rich: others were deliberately maimed by beggars to arouse compassion and extra alms. Even this latter crime was one upon which the law looked with a remarkably tolerant eye. In 1761 a beggar woman, convicted of deliberately 'putting out the eyes of children with who she went about the country' in order to attract pity and alms, was sentenced to no more than two years' imprisonment.

Text C is an extract from an anonymous eighteenth-century stage ballad.

> **Text C**
>
> 'Twas Saturday night, if I recollect right,
> When first I set out from London,
> I tickled a girl, her name it was Sall,
> And she and her brat were quite undone;
> The constable wrath, he took his staff,
> Thro' streets and thro' courts did me harass,
> So for fear of a fray, I took my body away,
> And she saddled her brat on the parish.

Text D is an extract from a 1771 reference book called *A Commentary on the Laws of England*, which defines the legal position of illegitimate children.

> **Text D**
>
> The rights are very few, being only such as he can *acquire*: for he can inherit nothing, being looked on as the son of nobody, and sometimes called *filius nullius*, sometimes *filius populi*. Yet he may gain a surname by reputation, though he has none by inheritance. . . . The incapacity of a bastard consists principally in this, that he cannot be heir to anyone, neither can he have heirs, but of his own body; for being *nullius filius*, he is therefore kin to nobody, and has no ancestor from who inheritable blood can be derived . . . really any other distinction, but just that of not inheriting, which civil policy renders necessary, would, with regard to the innocent offspring of his parents' crimes, be odious, unjust, and cruel to the last degree; and yet the civil law, so boasted of for its equitable decisions, made bastards in some cases incapable of even a gift from their parents.

Text E is an extract from *King Lear*, a tragedy by William Shakespeare written in about 1604.

Text E

Enter EDMUND, *with a letter.*

Thou, Nature, art my goddess; to thy law
My services are bound. Wherefore should I

Stand in the plague of custom, and permit
The curiosity of nations to deprive me,
For that I am some twelve or fourteen moonshines
Lag of a brother? Why bastard? Wherefore base?
When my dimensions are as well compact,
My mind as generous, and my shape as true,
As honest madam's issue? Why brand they us
With base? With baseness? Bastardy? Base, base?
Who in the lusty stealth of nature take
More composition and fierce quality
Than doth, within a dull, stale, tired bed,
Go to th' creating a whole tribe of fops,
Got 'tween asleep and wake? Well then,
Legitimate Edgar, I must have your land:
Our father's love is to the bastard Edmund
As to th' legitimate. Fine word 'legitimate'!
Well, my legitimate, if this letter speed,
And my invention thrive, Edmund the base
Shall top th' legitimate –: I grow, I prosper;
Now, gods, stand up for bastards!

Text F is an extract from an account of the lives of Brazilian street children published in 1989.

Text F

Twelve-year-old Teresa wandered barefoot into the hospital carrying a stinking bundle in her arms. She asked the doctors what was wrong with her child. They unwrapped the bundle and found a tiny, decomposing corpse. The baby was a month old; she had died of infections around her anus and her vagina. The acid of urine and faeces had corroded the flesh to such an extent that the bones stuck out. José Nelson de Freitas covered his face as he told me the story. 'She had never changed those filthy wrappings. Never once cleaned her child. She thought the baby was a doll! When we told her it was dead she sobbed and had nervous convulsions. We calmed her down with sedatives. Four hours later she slipped out of the hospital and went back to the square'.

Suggestions for Answer

The following suggestions for answer refer to only four of the six extracts above: you can analyse Texts C and F independently. Moreover, in an exercise such as this, the answers given here really are suggestions, since there is no fixed number of potential links. You could begin by comparing and contrasting similarities and differences of the following:

- Intended audience (student, theatre-goer, newspaper reader, lawyer, novel reader)
- Intended purpose or response (polemic to raise awareness, play to entertain, research to inform, explain and describe)
- Genre (fiction or non-fiction – novel, ballad, soliloquy, autobiography, legal document, report, historical monograph)
- Chronology/time frame (Elizabethan, eighteenth century, Victorian, contemporary – and one that is contemporary, but reports historical events)

J.K. Rowling was asked to write the foreword or introduction to a book published to raise funds for the National Council for One-Parent Families because of her then high-profile status as a single parent who apparently triumphed over the odds by becoming rich and famous. Ironically, Rowling uses her platform to challenge this media-inspired rags-to-riches myth, which she finds a simplistic cop-out or 'well-worn cliché'. In Rowling's Harry Potter books, the neglected hero magically defeats his enemies; real life, as she suggests to the adult readers of this text, is rather different.

Text A is an autobiographical account that concentrates on the grinding pettiness of a single parent's existence – baked beans, free nappies and charity shops – as a necessary corrective to the picturesque version peddled by the media. The fact that her readers have bought a book designed to raise funds for this particular charity shows that she is preaching to the converted; nevertheless, Rowling uses rhetorical devices to persuade them to share her sympathetic point of view. These include personal pronouns, three-part lists, statistics and humour; the extract begins with a comic comparison and ends with a powerful rule of three to emphasise her point. The presentation of this text makes it hard for the reader to adopt an **oppositional reading position** that challenges Rowling's supportive polemic grounded in the beliefs and expectations of modern liberal feminism.

Text B describes the brutality of everyday life for single mothers and their children in the eighteenth century. The writer uses the discourse structure of the impersonal factual recount. The pronouns are third person – 'she' and 'they' rather than Rowling's 'I' and 'you' – and he cites references, sources and dates to add credibility to his account. On the other hand, he also tells a good tale, adding interest to his narrative and creating sympathy with emotive lexis describing the horror of life on the streets for the disadvantaged: 'desperate', 'vicious', 'cruel', 'irregular passions', 'enslaved', 'criminal', 'maimed' and 'prostitution'. The use of shocking facts and interpretations tend to support a Marxist reading position in which society's economic and legal structures make it impossible for the disadvantaged and dispossessed to take advantage of the opportunities society has to offer.

Text D offers a clear, precise and technical definition of the legal status of an illegitimate child. The specialist jargon term 'nullius filius' (nobody's child) is used to classify illegitimacy in classic legal Latin, yet this dispassionate accuracy contrasts with a surprisingly forthright and passionate outburst against the 'incapacity of the bastard'. The inequalities that apply to illegitimate people are described as 'odious, unjust, and cruel to the last degree', and the writer argues that making children suffer for the actions of their parents is grotesquely unfair.

Edmund's **soliloquy** from *King Lear* (Text E) is a bold and confident statement of equality designed to contest the prevailing negative stereotype of the bastard in Shakespeare's time. In Jacobean England, society stigmatised and penalised unmarried mothers and their children very harshly, blaming them for all sorts of economic, cultural and religious problems. This harsh historical **context** may cause more sympathetic modern audiences to applaud Edmund's bravura speech rather than condemn it; we may read Edmund's amoral behaviour as stemming from a natural desire to challenge his treatment by society, rather than the result of innate evil. 'Now, gods, stand up for bastards' indeed. In short, all of the texts show a similar sympathetic response to the topic, but also a pattern of difference based upon their respective audiences, purposes and genres.

READING *BLEAK HOUSE* IN CONTEXT

As a reader, you will have responded to the above texts via a framework of ideas, values and opinions that affect how you read and receive them. The **dominant reading position** of most of these texts is sympathetic towards lone parents and their children and given this basic similarity, the topical link can be only a starting point. In order to make more sophisticated comparisons we need to look at the social, cultural and historical contexts of each text. The extra layers of meaning that can emerge when we read texts in context are shown in the extract below and the commentary that follows it. This extract is part of the narrative of Esther Summerson, the heroine of Charles Dickens's novel *Bleak House*, published in 1853.

> Dinner was over, and my godmother and I were sitting at the table by the fire. The clock ticked, the fire clicked; not another sound had been heard in the room, or in the house, for I don't know how long. I happened to look up timidly from my stitching across the table, at my godmother, and I saw in her face, looking gloomily at me, 'It would have been far better, little Esther, that you had no birthday; that you had not been born!'
>
> I broke out crying and sobbing, and I said 'O, dear godmother, tell me, pray do tell me, did mama die on my birthday?'

continued

'No,' she returned, 'Ask me no more, child!'

'O, do pray tell me something of her. Do now, at last, dear godmother, if you please! What did I do to her? How did I lose her? Why am I so different from other children, and why is it my fault, dear godmother? No, no, no, don't go away. O, speak to me!'

I was in a kind of fright beyond my grief; and I caught hold of her dress, and was kneeling to her. She had been saying all the while, 'Let me go!' But now she stood still.

Her darkened face had such power over me, that it stopped me in the midst of my vehemence, I put up my trembling little hand to clasp hers, or to beg her pardon with what earnestness I might, but withdrew it as she looked at me, and laid it on my fluttering heart. She raised me, sat in her chair, and standing me before her, said, slowly, in a cold, low voice – I see her knitted brow, and pointed finger:

'Your mother, Esther, is your disgrace, and you are hers. The time will come – and soon enough – when you will understand this better, and feel it too, as no one save a woman can. I have forgiven her' – but her face did not relent – 'the wrong she did to me, and I say no more of it, though it was greater than you will ever know – that anyone will ever know, but I, the sufferer. For yourself, unfortunate girl, orphaned and degraded from the first of these evil anniversaries, pray daily that the sins of others be not visited upon your head according to what is written. Forget your mother and leave all other people to forget her who will do her unhappy child that greatest kindness. Now, go!'

She checked me, however, as I was about to depart from her – so frozen as I was! – and added this:

'Submission, self-denial, diligent work, are the preparations for a life begun with such a shadow on it. You are different from other children, Esther, because you were not born, like them, in common sinfulness and wrath. You are set apart.'

I went up to my room, and crept into bed, and laid my doll's cheek against mine wet with tears; and holding that solitary friend upon my bosom, cried myself to sleep. Imperfect as my understanding of my sorrow was, I knew that I had brought no joy, at any time, to anybody's heart, and that I was to no one upon earth what Dolly was to me.

Dear, dear, to think how much time we passed along together afterwards, and how often I repeated to the doll the story of my birthday, and confided to her that I would try, as hard as ever I could, to repair the fault I had been born with (of which I confessedly felt guilty yet innocent), and would strive as I grew up to be industrious, contented and kind-hearted, and to do some good to some one, and win some love to myself if I could. I hope it is not self-indulgent to shed these tears as I think of it. I am very thankful, I am very cheerful, but I cannot quite help their coming to my eyes.

When this text was written in 1853, it was almost impossible for women to avoid being categorised as one of two polarised stereotypes – the pure and virtuous domestic 'angel in the house' or the sexually predatory fallen woman. These binary opposites were characterised with reference to the two biblical Marys closest to Jesus: his mother, the idealised Madonna, and the prostitute Mary Magdalene. These extreme contemporary ideas about women are reflected in mid-Victorian fiction in general and the work of Dickens in particular.

Bleak House was originally published in serial instalments in a magazine edited and published by Dickens himself. It is a complex and densely plotted novel in which an **omniscient narrator** tells half the story, while the other half is presented through the eyes of an **unreliable narrator**, a young woman called Esther Summerson. Point of view and narrative structure are therefore crucial to an understanding of the novel. Although Esther narrates about half the novel, when she is not supposed to have witnessed a particular episode, it makes no sense for Dickens to use her to report it. On the other hand, in Esther's absence, the all-seeing narrator is free to swoop down on any character or event at any time in order to bring things into focus. As a result, the reader is faced with differentiating between *Bleak House*'s two narrators. Esther is a fictional construct, but this does not imply that the other **narrative voice** is necessarily that of Charles Dickens. The narrator's voice blends in with other voices in a story, reporting on other characters. Narrators are selective; they may gloss, rearrange or edit actual events (real or imagined) in order to present their chosen version. While Esther is involved in the events she is reporting, the other **narrative persona** is an external observer. In the novel, the way Esther lives her life – as both an individual and as a representative of Victorian womanhood – allows Dickens to examine her illegitimacy as a potentially disabling psychological condition, a complex social issue and a central woman question. Social pressure (personified by her terrifying aunt) leads Esther to feel not just that her life is not worth living, but that it is a life that should never have begun.

Dickens presents Esther's illegitimacy as the reason why she is cut off from many important social and cultural spheres, but a feminist reading of *Bleak House* might interpret her abused, marginalised and isolated status as applicable to the social position of Victorian women in general. A Marxist reading would see society's response to and definition of the family as saying a lot about its moral and sexual concerns. The exaggerated importance attached to marriage in Victorian England encouraged a climate of opinion in which people who appeared to threaten that sacred institution (such as adulterers, prostitutes, unmarried mothers or illegitimate children) were demonised and scapegoated. From this oppositional reading position we might query the vested interest of the upper and middle classes in upholding strict laws about property, hierarchy and inheritance. As the Victorian ideology of the family located sex strictly within the confines of marriage, alternative relationships were condemned.

The ironic tension that exists between the two contrasting narrative voices of the novel – one apparently masculine, bitter and angry, the other feminine, mild and passive – is its key organisational feature. Structurally and metaphorically, Esther Summerson is a **liminal** figure within the text, hovering on the threshold that divides 'respectable' society from the outsiders, and questioning the criteria by which she is judged and excluded.

In terms of the plot, the existence of an illegitimate child functions as the classic family secret; a convenient skeleton in the cupboard that the writer can use to engineer the downfall of an apparently respectable family like the Dedlocks in *Bleak House*. Illegitimacy was a useful device for writers producing long novels that were originally part works, as they needed ongoing hidden secrets (and potential cliffhangers) to keep their readers hooked. Beyond the plot level, however, the theme was a cipher for wider concerns about women, sex, class, power, money and the law. Dickens was one of the first writers to write sympathetically about illegitimacy while still using the concept as a structural device to explore the danger zone of human sexual relationships, which included seduction, adultery and rape.

CHOOSING YOUR OWN THEME

If you wish to extend your literary study of the theme of single parents, these texts will get you started:

Novels

The Scarlet Letter Nathaniel Hawthorne
No Name Wilkie Collins
Silas Marner and *Adam Bede* George Eliot
Poor Cow and *Up the Junction* Nell Dunn
About a Boy Nick Hornby

Plays

A Woman of No Importance Oscar Wilde
A Taste of Honey Shelagh Delaney

If you decide to choose your own theme, assess the basis of your comparison carefully before you start planning your work. Decide on a topic that will allow you to focus on the techniques and methods each writer uses to explore it. Ask yourself if your chosen theme is sufficiently complex and challenging: uncertainty and instability will give you plenty of things to write about, whereas dull and routine essays can emerge when you are too sure of your ground. A Level literature students interested in the theme of family relationships have successfully compared the following texts:

Silas Marner (George Eliot) and *About a Boy* (Nick Hornby): the role of the foster father; two novels

Great Expectations (Charles Dickens) and *The Importance of Being Earnest* (Oscar Wilde): the theme of the foundling child; novel and play

Frankenstein (Mary Shelley) and *The Fifth Child* (Doris Lessing): parent-and-child relationships where the child is physically and/or psychologically damaged in some sense; two novels

Sense and Sensibility (Jane Austen) and *The Daughters of the Late Colonel* (Katherine Mansfield): sister relationships; novel and short story

Other interesting themes to compare include the following:

Marriage/Role of Women

Any novel by Jane Austen
Middlemarch George Eliot
The Awakening Kate Chopin
Lady Audley's Secret Mary Braddon
Pygmalion George Bernard Shaw
Educating Rita Willy Russell
The Yellow Wallpaper/Turned Charlotte Perkins Gillman
Short stories by Kate Chopin, Katherine Mansfield, Flannery O'Connor, Carson McCullers, Angela Carter

The American Dream

An American Tragedy Theodore Dreiser
The Great Gatsby F. Scott Fitzgerald
The Grapes of Wrath/Of Mice and Men John Steinbeck
American Psycho Bret Easton Ellis
The Secret History Donna Tartt
A View from the Bridge/All My Sons Arthur Miller
A Streetcar Named Desire Tennessee Williams
Who's Afraid of Virginia Woolf? Edward Albee

Growing Up (*Bildungsroman*)

Jane Eyre Charlotte Brontë
Great Expectations/David Copperfield Charles Dickens
Huckleberry Finn Mark Twain
The Catcher in the Rye J.D. Salinger

continued

Vernon God Little D.B.C. Pierre
Oranges Are Not the Only Fruit Jeanette Winterson
The Color Purple Alice Walker
I Know Why the Caged Bird Sings Maya Angelou
Bad Blood Lorna Sage

War

The Red Badge of Courage Stephen Crane
Goodbye to All That Robert Graves
Birdsong Sebastian Faulks
Regeneration Pat Barker
Journey's End R.C. Sheriff
The Long and the Short and the Tall Willis Hall

The best-known First World War poets are Wilfred Owen, Siegfried Sassoon and Rupert Brooke. If you choose to compare poems and prose or drama, bear in mind that you must study a wide enough selection to bear the weight of a comparison with a much longer text.

CONCLUSION

This chapter has shown that thematic links between texts provide a way into a comparative exploration of language and form, interpretations of text and various contextual factors. Comparing and contrasting different writers' approaches to a particular subject reveal aspects of style and structure that might otherwise go unnoticed. By using a theme as a starting point, you can develop the comparison by examining how and why your chosen writers have dealt with the topic in order to understand what the central idea may have meant to them. You have responded to the single-parent texts in this chapter, and perhaps guessed at what has been left unsaid. You have formed an impression about the voice in each text – ironic, moralistic, passionate, detached, scientific, rational, angry, bitter or amused. In examining these texts about single-parent families we can look at various writers' interpretations of a topic that is both a simple fact of life and a potential metaphor for the preoccupations, norms and values of the societies in which they lived.

SUMMARY

This chapter has done the following:

- Discussed the notion of connecting texts thematically
- Linked a variety of texts on the same theme
- Compared those texts in terms of audience, purpose, genre and context
- Investigated the social, cultural and historical contexts of one response to the theme in detail
- Considered various factors relevant to choosing an appropriate theme for comparison
- Suggested several possible literary texts and themes that might be successfully compared

LINKED AND LABELLED TEXTS   CHAPTER 3

This chapter compares texts that have already been linked and labelled. Comparing texts organised in this way means studying the period in which a group of writers lived and the circumstances surrounding their work in order to assess their similarities and differences.

LABELLING TEXTS

Before we begin to examine a particular group of linked texts, however, we need to consider the whole idea of labelling texts in the first place, as cataloguing texts is a process that raises many important questions.

Exercise 1 – Discussion

Discuss the following questions about grouping texts with the rest of your class. Suggestions for answer follow.

- Who attaches labels to texts?
- What sorts of labels are they?
- Where do the labels come from?
- Why are they used?
- Who benefits from the process?
- Are these labels removable or permanent?
- What are the possible effects of labelling for writers and readers?

Suggestions for Answer

Traditionally, literary labels (such as Modernism, the Theatre of the Absurd or the Metaphysical Poets; look them up if you wish) have been attached to certain texts by influential journalists, critics and academics. Parcelling up texts and attaching labels to them help teachers organise courses and librarians shelve books; they can also reinforce ideas about what counts as Great Literature. These labels tend to last for a long time.

THE GREAT TRADITION AND CULTURAL CAPITAL

For many years, studying English Literature meant reading a **canon** of great literary works by great writers who were seen to have buried priceless nuggets of meaning at the heart of their works of genius. The reader's role was to extract this precious core like scientists isolating DNA. The meaning of a text was seen as fixed and absolute, and the teacher's role was to point out the significance of this meaning to their students, rather than enabling students to make meanings of their own.

After two world wars (1914–18 and 1939–45), influential critics such as Cambridge professor F.R. Leavis argued that good books had a moral dimension that could heal or even civilise society. If pupils at school had to read great literature, they might learn how to live better lives. The individual circumstances and experiences of readers were not an issue: their role was to be passive rather than active – accepting rather than creating meaning. Great (and almost invariably dead) writers were to be discovered and worshipped, rather than investigated and challenged.

In his book *The Great Tradition*, written in the 1940s, Leavis argued that only four writers were really significant contributors to the development of the classic English novel – Jane Austen, George Eliot, Henry James and Joseph Conrad. This concept of an élite squad of geniuses persists today: Professor Harold Bloom describes Geoffrey Chaucer as 'second only to Shakespeare'. Judging writers' performances as if they are players in a kind of Eng. Lit. Premiership football division is not always helpful.

An alternative theory about literature was the concept of **cultural capital**. The Marxist critic Raymond Williams felt that far from helping to improve and unite society, the Leavis approach might shore up social discrimination by creating an 'us and them' split between popular (working class) culture and high (middle and upper class) culture. If cultural capital represents your personal stake in society – the extent to which you fit in – then some people may be exposed to subtle but powerful pressures, which reinforce the idea that while they can read Catherine Cookson, they cannot read Charles Dickens, and that while they might go to the theatre to watch a pantomime, they will not go to see *Macbeth*. From the cultural capital perspective, labelling may seem a snobbish way of protecting élite or classic texts from exposure to ordinary people. It is unlikely that writers want to be parcelled up and pigeonholed like this – particularly not those such as the Romantics, who will be the focus of this chapter.

PROBLEMS WITH THE LABELLING PROCESS

Think about other things that can be labelled – types of popular music, say, or designer clothes. In the 1990s, the music media identified a new phenomenon, which became known as Britpop. Even while they asserted their individuality, the names of many of the most prominent bands tell a different story, sharing a monosyllabic similarity – Blur, Pulp, Suede. And though much of the publicity that surrounds such new cultural movements may turn out to be hype or myth, maybe our desire to recognise 'the next big thing' shows how seriously we take art, music and literature. The whole point about being radical is to be original – but circumstances may insist upon stressing your links to others. Artists are usually well aware of what their contemporaries are doing – but we risk tidying writers up too much if we become label-fixated. This process can be compared to people who wear only designer label clothes – their choice is restricted and they risk paying too much for cheap fakes. Moreover, even genuine designer goods can be poor quality and over-priced: labels need checking, and should not override independent judgement. In any case, literary reputations (like fashions in music and clothes) are clearly not fixed over time – so although Charles Dickens is still widely read and studied today, his friend and contemporary Edward Bulwer Lytton is almost unknown. Conversely another of Dickens's associates, Wilkie Collins, fell out of favour for years – but his novels have now been reprinted and he is mainstream once more.

Before examining some literary texts, we will pursue the idea of why and how groups form a bit further. These three non-fiction extracts are all concerned with the development and operation of groups in general and two well-known twentieth-century youth cults – goths and punks – in particular.

Exercise 2 – Social Groups and Youth Subcultures

- Identify the genres of each of the following texts and explain how and why you have classified them
- Compare what each text has to say about groups and labelling

Suggestions for answer follow on page 32.

Text A is an extract from a textbook for A Level Communication Studies students. The words printed in bold are as printed in the original.

Text A

Each of us inevitably belongs to a variety of groups.

You could list those groups you joined from your own choice, for example, a youth club or a pop group. You could also list those groups you joined without a free choice, for example, your family or your school. There are many different sorts of groups with different sorts of purposes. They cater for our different needs. These needs may be short-term (an evening party) or long-term (a club that we belong to). It is interesting to consider why we join and form various groupings.

continued

The word 'group' can carry many different meanings and associations. **It is helpful to describe different types of groups according to their functions and qualities**. We have just noted that some are short-lived gatherings of people and others are more permanent gatherings. Some are formal, others informal. Some are small (say, five people), others are large (say, several hundred). Some are local, others international. People in a group have some interest or purpose in common which brings them together.

Although **individuals in a group share common interests**, these people may not always share all of themselves. Having agreed on some purposes, people may disagree fiercely about how these purposes should be achieved. They might disagree on how the group should be organised. Some members may want all members to be equal, but other members may prefer to have a designated leader for others to follow. When people gather together there is usually some sort of struggle for power.

Relationships and patterns of communication have to be developed for the group to function. **If there is no interaction between the individuals then a group cannot be formed**.

Text B is an extract from a sociological study of youth subcultures.

Text B

[Punk] undermined every relevant discourse. Thus dancing, usually an involving and expressive medium in British rock and mainstream pop cultures, was turned into a dumbshow of blank robotics.

The music was similarly distinguished from mainstream rock and pop. It was uniformly basic and direct in its appeal, whether through intention or lack of expertise. If the latter, then the punks certainly made a virtue of necessity ('We want to be amateurs' – Johnny Rotten). Typically, a barrage of guitars with the volume and treble turned to maximum accompanied by the occasional saxophone would pursue relentless (un)melodic lines against a turbulent background of cacophonous drumming and screamed vocals. Johnny Rotten succinctly defined punk's position on harmonics: 'We're into chaos not music.'

The names of the groups (the Unwanted, the Rejects, the Sex Pistols, the Clash, the Worst, etc.) and the titles of the songs e.g. 'I Wanna be Sick on You', reflected the tendency towards wilful desecration and the voluntary assumption of outcast status which characterised the whole punk movement.

Such tactics were, to adapt Levi-Strauss's famous phrase, 'things to whiten mother's hair with'.

Most notably, there was an attempt, the first by a predominantly working-class youth culture, to provide an alternative critical space within the subculture itself to counteract the hostile or at least ideologically inflected coverage which punk was receiving in the media. The existence of an alternative punk press demonstrated that it was not only clothes or music that could be immediately and cheaply produced from the limited resources at hand. The fanzines (*Sniffin Glue, Ripped and Torn*, etc.) were journals edited by an individual or a group, consisting of reviews, editorials and interviews with prominent punks, produced on a small scale as cheaply as possible, stapled together and distributed through a small number of sympathetic retail outlets.

The language in which the various manifestos were framed was determinedly 'working class' (i.e. it was liberally peppered with swear words) and typing errors and grammatical mistakes, misspellings and jumbled pagination were left uncorrected in the final proof. Those corrections were left to be deciphered by the reader. The overwhelming impression was one of urgency and immediacy, of a paper produced in indecent haste, of memos from the front line.

Text C is an extract from a review of a television comedy programme about goths.

Text C

To begin with, goths do not like being called goths. They prefer the label 'industrialist', though they will make a point of telling you that they hate labels. This is a bit rich coming from a group of people whose attitude to clothes, books, art and life in general is as mindlessly off-the-peg as a Burton's closing-down sale. If they can't be labelled then what can? Ask a goth who is their favourite modern painter, and they won't plump for Picasso, Miro or Matisse, they will invariably go for Salvador Dali. That is because goths, despite their moody pretensions to depth and amoral intellect, need everything spelt out to them. And no artist before or since has so laboriously and hamfistedly spelt out 'weird' like Dali did. Of course, if they had any sense of discrimination they would at least choose somebody of the calibre of Edvard Munch. But on planet goth, discrimination boils down to infantile notions of light, dark, life, death, black and white.

Take their taste in literature. If they own books at all, and regrettably a fair few of them do, then they will be the complete and well-thumbed works of Anne

continued

Rice (self-styled 'Queen of the Damned' and the undead's answer to Jeffrey Archer), the collected works of Byron (unread but there because he looked a bit like a goth), William Burroughs (also unread, but then Burroughs took heroin, hung out with Yank goth Lydia Lunch and shot his wife, which is cool), the Marquis de Sade (because he tortured people and had a silly haircut) and anything that mentions the womanising, racist, mass-murdering bastard Charles Manson. Their taste in jewellery begins and ends with silver skulls and upside-down crosses, normally hammered through some particularly sensitive part of their anatomy. If a goth owns a pet, it will be something thick, surly, vaguely dangerous and usually sporting either scales or eight legs.

Suggestions for Answer

All these texts are examples of non-literary material about the formation and regulation of social groups, yet while Texts A and B are formal, academic and neutral in tone, Text C is colloquial, comic and biased. Texts B and C describe the features of two well-known and highly specific youth subcultures (punks and goths) in some detail, whereas Text A is a generalised, informative overview of group communication theory. Text B is interesting because of the clash between the formal discourse structure and the outrageous subject matter; its smooth and fluent style provides an ironic contrast with the chaotic and anarchic textual (dis)organ-isation of the punk fanzines it describes. It functions as a halfway house between the textbook and the comic article. Text C's voice is flippant and outrageous; the collocation of the Marquis de Sade's bad hair cut and predilection for mass torture presents these two crimes as moral equivalents, which further stresses the facile superficiality of goth culture. A wide frame of goth cultural reference is included, but the painters mentioned are criticised as talentless, and the writers' books are only for show. The picture presented is a compendium of recognisable clichés – grotesquely unfair and exaggerated, but therefore a rich source of potential comedy for anyone who is not a member of the group being ridiculed. The generic structures of groups and groupings established scientifically in Text A mutate via an unusually erudite analysis of the punk movement into a highly personal postcard from planet goth, yet all three extracts relate to the central idea of defining ourselves in terms of our personal and social relationships.

CASE STUDY: THE ROMANTIC MOVEMENT

Text A above takes it for granted that whereas most people belong to some groups by choice, there are other groups of which you are automatically a member, such as your family. The rest of this chapter will consider ways of comparing a variety of writers in the context of **Romanticism**, and as you read, ask yourself what kind of group you think they are. In other words, did they join a new artistic movement, or were they tagged as members without their permission, perhaps even after their deaths? Think about the potential strengths and weaknesses of the labelling process as you work through this chapter. Other questions to consider when comparing members of any literary group are as follows:

- Did they form part of a united movement and work together at the time?
- Did contemporary critics and reviewers identify them as a collective?
- Did they adopt independent positions within the framework of the group?
- Can writers be misread because they are compared with others?
- Do literary groups allow readers to see writers in their proper perspective, or do we risk seeing only what we expect to see?
- Did being part of a movement mean that the members admired each other – or did they argue or even become rivals?
- To what extent do writers (among others) use the press and the media to publicise their ideas and advertise themselves, and then complain that they have been pigeonholed?

THE ROMANTIC BACKGROUND AND THE AGE OF REVOLUTION

Romanticism was a European cultural phenomenon encompassing not only literature (in all its forms) but also art, music, politics, philosophy, science and religion. Spanning roughly the years 1770 to 1840, Romanticism was set against a historical background of radical change in which traditional social, religious, economic and political beliefs were challenged and reinterpreted. The established **Enlightenment** ideal of logical, systematic progress gave way to an unstable revolutionary age. Previously sacrosanct ideas were vulnerable, and so, for instance, when the number of people who were unhappy with the concept of an all-powerful ruler appointed by God reached a critical mass, the King of France was guillotined and an absolute monarchy was replaced with a democratic republic.

Most writers, artists and musicians did not call themselves Romantics at the time: the term materialised with the benefit of hindsight and critical perspective. In this sense, the Romantics probably resembled one of the looser groupings referred to in Text A above, rather than the self-defining goth in-crowd. Nevertheless, many writers did share certain core values and ideas, especially the belief that artists should seek the essential truth about life. Personal experiences and perceptions were paramount; far from seeing their role as mirroring life, the Romantics wanted to interpret life and mediate it through personal experience.

THE BYRONIC HERO

Romantic writers were often seen (and tended to see themselves) as anti-Establishment figures existing on the margins of mainstream society – like the punks and goths described earlier. One of the recurrent **motifs** of Romanticism is the wandering outcast, an excluded figure on the threshold of respectable society who questions its values and ideas. This Romantic **archetype** is often referred to as the **Byronic hero**, after the poet George Gordon, Lord Byron (1788–1824), a legendary figure who defied conventional morality and authority.

Byron's significance as a cultural **icon** is the legacy not only of his poetry, but of a life lived as a series of symbolic contradictions and paradoxes. His public image played as great a role in his success as did his poetry, and his experience of the cycle of celebrity is eerily close to the rise and fall of modern pop and film stars. Though Byron was extremely handsome, his physical disability (a deformed foot) cast a shadow over his life and work. Acclaimed by literary London, he was run out of town when rumours spread about his unorthodox love life: he had abused his wife, had an affair with his half-sister and was sexually attracted to young boys. By 1816 he was living a nomadic life abroad, in permanent exile from England. An aristocrat who took his seat in the House of Lords, he died at Missolonghi in Greece in 1824, supporting the cause of an independent republic; trying, in a sense, to translate the theory of Romantic nationalism into practice.

Byron created an image of himself which proved hugely influential both during his own lifetime and for generations to come. The word 'Romantic' is linked to the French word *roman*, meaning a novel or story, and implies a search for meaning and identity. From living in poverty in a small flat above a shop in Aberdeen, at the age of ten Byron inherited a title, an ancestral home and a history. This transformation influenced the rest of his life.

Byron travelled extensively and began to develop global political and artistic perspectives very different from the patronising view of other cultures held by most of his English contemporaries. Like many Romantics, his hero was Napoleon Bonaparte. At first Napoleon was seen as an idealistic young leader whose rule would spread the ideals of liberty, equality and fraternity throughout Europe and beyond; his rise from obscure poverty to military genius and saviour of republican France made him the emblem of the Romantic man of action. However, when Napoleon declared himself Emperor and began to act just like the representatives of the hated monarchy overthrown in 1793, the Romantics became disillusioned. By 1814, when Byron wrote his *Ode to Napoleon*, Bonaparte was a tainted hero. The leader who redrew the map of Europe was reinterpreted as a fallen idol, brought down not only by lesser men, but also by the tragic flaws in his own character. Byron commemorated the decline of a man whose career path seemed to foreshadow his own; Napoleon was exiled after his defeat at Waterloo in 1815, and a year later Byron fled the scandal about to engulf him at home.

Over time, Byron's flight and exile has come to symbolise the Romantic quest for freedom, mobility and space. His behaviour now seems to be interpreted as acceptable if unorthodox, whereas a different version of his story could present him as a dangerous paedophile or pervert. Towards the end of his short life, his status as a displaced person led him to try to reconnect with patriotic Romanticism in action. His devotion to the cause of Greek independence cost him his life, but made him an inspirational Romantic archetype – the freedom fighter of passion and intellect. The relationship between Byron himself and the heroic outlaws he created has fascinated many readers of his work. Fiona McCarthy's biography *Byron: Life and Legend* (2003) is an absorbing study of the man and his myth.

Exercise 3 – Authorial Contexts: Byron Poem

Read the following text and look for links between the details of the life of Lord Byron given above and the subject matter of his poem. Suggestions for answer follow on page 36.

George Gordon, Lord Byron

On This Day I Complete My 36th Year (1824)

'Tis time this heart should be unmoved,
    Since others it hath ceased to move:
Yet, though I cannot be beloved,
    Still let me love!

My days are in the yellow leaf;
    The flowers and fruits of love are gone;
The worm, the canker, and the grief
    Are mine alone!

The fire that on my bosom preys
    Is lone as some volcanic isle;
No torch is kindled at its blaze –
    A funeral pile.

The hope, the fear, the jealous care,
    The exalted portion of the pain
And power of love, I cannot share,
    But wear the chain.

But 'tis not *thus* – and 'tis not *here* –
    Such thoughts should shake my soul, nor now,
Where glory decks the hero's bier,
    Or binds his brow.

The sword, the banner, and the field,
    Glory and Greece, around me see!
The Spartan, borne upon his shield,
    Was not more free.

continued

Awake! (not Greece – she *is* awake!)
    Awake, my spirit! Think through *whom*
Thy life-blood tracks its parent lake,
    And then strike home!

Tread those reviving passions down,
    Unworthy manhood! – unto thee
Indifferent should the smile or frown
    Of beauty be.

If thou regrett'st thy youth, *why live?*
    The land of honourable death
Is here: – up to the field, and give
    Away thy breath!

Seek out – less often sought than found –
    A soldier's grave, for thee the best;
Then look around, and choose thy ground,
    And take thy rest!

                    MISSOLONGHI, Jan. 22, 1824

Suggestions for Answer

Byron lived the concept of the Romantic hero as well as writing it, and this text unites the concept of the doomed hero in art as well as life, since he died at Missolonghi, where the poem was written. In a sense, therefore, our interpretation of this text is affected by an event which took place after its production. The depth of Byron's passion for Greece, personified as a goddess-like figure of liberty, is clear. But once such a rebel has been rubber-stamped as a literary icon, has he not been reabsorbed by the society which once excluded him? Can you still be an outsider when your work appears on examination syllabuses and university courses all over the world? Ironically, Byron did not earn the 'soldier's grave' of the final stanza: he died of fever, having never seen 'the sword, the banner and the field'. It is fair to say, however, that the text's references to 'a funeral pile' and 'the hero's bier' seem eerily appropriate.

ROMANTIC TEXTS IN CONTEXT

Many other Romantics also interpreted the symbolic touchstone figure of the lonely wanderer and the rest of this chapter will use this motif as a way into examining some contexts for comparing linked texts. It would be helpful to do some research first in order to assess how far the following texts may be seen as typically Romantic or representative of the social, cultural, economic, artistic, political climate of the time.

Exercise 4 – Research

Find out as much as possible about the lives and work of the following writers and any important links which exist between them. You will find this information in a library or on the Internet. Your class could share out the workload and present the findings to each other. One of these writers is not usually associated with the Romantic movement; find out who and why.

- William Blake (1757–1827)
- William Wordsworth (1770–1850)
- Samuel Taylor Coleridge (1772–1834)
- Jane Austen (1775–1817)
- John Keats (1795–1821)
- Percy Bysshe Shelley (1792–1822)
- Mary Shelley (1797–1851)

There are no suggestions for answer for this exercise.

KEY CONTEXTUAL QUESTIONS

Bear in mind the importance of context when reading the texts in this chapter. The context of time refers to the fact that contemporary writers lived and worked in a similar social, cultural and historical setting, and you know something of the background to the Romantic period. The context of production suggests that links will exist between texts made by a group of people with something in common, even if they didn't think of themselves as a partnership at the time. However, as well as studying the dominant ideologies and values of their culture and the extent to which they supported or challenged the status quo, when comparing the work of the Romantics, the following contextual questions are also relevant:

- Is the text part of an anthology or poetry collection? This could be contemporary, such as *Lyrical Ballads* by Wordsworth and Coleridge, or modern, such as *The Penguin Book of Romantic Poetry*.
- Did other people contribute to the text? Wordsworth used his sister Dorothy's journals and nature notes as inspiration for some of his poetry, and Percy Shelley wrote the introduction for his wife Mary's *Frankenstein*.
- Does the text refer to or make use of other texts? *Frankenstein* refers to or quotes from works by Wordsworth, Shelley, Byron and others.
- Has a specific social, political or cultural event sparked off an artistic reaction? Percy Shelley responded to the Peterloo Massacre (when government soldiers

broke up a peaceful demonstration by a crowd of poor weavers, killing and injuring many) with his satire *The Masque of Anarchy* and Byron's poetry is full of references to contemporary events.

- Does the text refer to other writers? Shelley's *Adonais* mourns the tragically early death of his friend John Keats.
- Were there significant personal relationships or partnerships between writers? The friendship of Wordsworth and Coleridge, the marriage of Percy and Mary Shelley and, above all, Byron's legendary house party for the Shelleys at the Villa Diodati are relevant here.

Exercise 5 – Comparing Romantic Texts

Compare the methods used by each writer to present the theme of the isolated wanderer, and try to assess the extent to which you feel the Romantic label is appropriate.

Suggestions for answer are at the back of the back of the book.

Text A

William Wordsworth

Old Man Travelling (1798)
[Animal tranquillity and decay, a sketch]

The little hedgerow birds,
That peck along the road, regard him not.
He travels on, and in his face, his step,
His gait, is one expression; every limb,
His look and bending figure, all bespeak
A man who does not move with pain, but moves
With thought – He is insensibly subdued
To settled quiet: he is one by whom
All effort seems forgotten, one to whom
Long patience has such mild composure given,
That patience now doth seem a thing, of which
He hath no need. He is by nature led
To peace so perfect, that the young behold
With envy, what the old man hardly feels.
– I asked him whither he was bound, and what
The object of his journey; he replied
'Sir! I am going many miles to take
A last leave of my son, a mariner,
Who from a sea-fight has been brought to Falmouth,
And there is dying in an hospital.'

Text B

Jane Austen

Sense and Sensibility (1811)

Sixteen-year-old Marianne Dashwood lives with her widowed mother and two sisters, Elinor and Margaret. Unlike sensible, practical Elinor, Marianne is a romantic dreamer, in love with the idea of finding true love. In this extract, she has an accident while out walking in the countryside with her younger sister, Margaret.

A gentleman carrying a gun, with two pointers playing around him, was passing up the hill and within a few yards of Marianne, when her accident happened. He put down his gun and ran to her assistance. She had raised herself from the ground, but her foot had been twisted in the fall, and she was scarcely able to stand. The gentleman offered his services, and perceiving that her modesty declined what her situation rendered necessary, took her up in his arms without farther delay, and carried her down the hill. Then passing through the garden, the gate of which had been left open by Margaret, he bore her directly into the house, whither Margaret was just arrived, and quitted not his hold till he had seated her in a chair in the parlour.

Elinor and her mother rose up in amazement at their entrance, and while the eyes of both were fixed on him with an evident wonder and a secret admiration which equally sprung from his appearance, he apologized for his intrusion by relating its cause, in a manner so frank and so graceful, that his person, which was uncommonly handsome, received additional charms from his voice and expression. Had he been even old, ugly and vulgar, the gratitude and kindness of Mrs. Dashwood would have been secured by any act of attention to her child; but the influence of youth, beauty, and elegance, gave an interest to the action which came home to her feelings.

She thanked him again and again; and with a sweetness of address that always attended her, invited him to be seated. But this he declined, as he was dirty and wet. Mrs. Dashwood then begged to know to whom she was obliged. His name, he replied, was Willoughby, and his present home was at Allenham, from whence he hoped she would allow him the honour of calling to-morrow to enquire after Miss Dashwood. The honour was readily granted, and he then departed, to make himself still more interesting, in the midst of a heavy rain.

His manly beauty and more than common gracefulness were instantly the theme of general admiration, and the laugh which his gallantry raised against Marianne, received particular spirit from his exterior attractions. Marianne herself had seen

continued

less of his person than the rest, for the confusion which crimsoned over her face, on his lifting her up, had robbed her of the power of regarding him after their entering the house. But she had seen enough of him to join in all the admiration of the others, and with an energy which always adorned her praise. His person and air were equal to what her fancy had ever drawn for the hero of a favourite story; and in his carrying her into the house with so little previous formality, there was a rapidity of thought which particularly recommended the action to her. Every circumstance belonging to him was interesting. His name was good, his residence was in their favourite village, and she soon found out that of all manly dresses a shooting-jacket was the most becoming. Her imagination was busy, her reflections were pleasant, and the pain of a sprained ancle was disregarded.

Text C

P.B. Shelley

Ozymandias (1817)

'I met a traveller from an antique land
Who said: Two vast and trunkless legs of stone
Stand in the desert . . . Near them, on the sand,
Half sunk, a shattered visage lies, whose frown,
And wrinkled lip, and sneer of cold command,
Tell that its sculptor well those passions read
Which yet survive, stamped on these lifeless things,
The hand that mocked them, and the hand that fed;
And on the pedestal these words appear:
"My name is Ozymandias, king of kings:
Look on my works, ye Mighty, and despair!"
Nothing besides remains. Round the decay
Of that colossal wreck, boundless and bare
The lone and level sands stretch far away.'

Text D

Mary Shelley

Frankenstein (1818)

In this extract, the creature tells his creator, Victor Frankenstein, about his growing sense of alienation from 'normal' society. He has read several books, including not only John Milton's epic religious poem *Paradise Lost*, but also, crucially, the diary Victor kept while he was actually making the creature in his laboratory.

Paradise Lost excited different and far deeper emotions. I read it, as I had read the other volumes that had fallen into my hands, as a true history. It moved every feeling of wonder and awe that the picture of an omnipotent God warring with his creatures was capable of exciting. I often referred the several situations, as their similarity struck me, to my own. Like Adam, I was apparently united by no link to any other being in existence, but his state was far different from mine in every other respect. He had come forth from the hands of God, a perfect creature, happy and prosperous, guarded by the especial care of his Creator; he was allowed to converse with, and acquire knowledge from, beings of a superior nature: but I was wretched, helpless, and alone. Many times I considered Satan as the fitter emblem of my condition; for often, like him, when I viewed the bliss of my protectors, the bitter gall of envy rose within me.

Another circumstance strengthened and confirmed these feelings. Soon after my arrival in the hovel, I discovered some papers in the pocket of the dress which I had taken from your laboratory. At first I had neglected them; but now that I was able to decipher the characters in which they were written, I began to study them with diligence. It was your journal of the four months that preceded my creation. You minutely described in these papers every step you took in the progress of your work; this history was mingled with accounts of domestic occurrences. You, doubtless, recollect these papers. Here they are. Everything is related in them which bears reference to my accursed origin; the whole detail of that series of disgusting circumstances which produced it is set in view; the minutest description of my odious and loathsome person is given, in language which painted your own horrors and rendered mine indelible. I sickened as I read. 'Hateful day when I received life!' I exclaimed in agony. 'Accursed creator! Why did you form a monster so hideous that even you turned away from me in disgust? God, in pity, made man beautiful and alluring, after his own image; but my form is a filthy type of yours, more horrid even from the very resemblance. Satan had his companions, fellow-devils, to admire and encourage him; but I am solitary and abhorred.'

EXTENSION EXERCISE: ROMANTIC REFLECTIONS IN *THE RIME OF THE ANCIENT MARINER*

The Rime of the Ancient Mariner, a narrative poem by Samuel Taylor Coleridge, could be compared with the other Romantic texts in this chapter. *The Ancient Mariner* was first published in *Lyrical Ballads*, a collaboration between Coleridge and his friend William Wordsworth. *Old Man Travelling* also appeared in this volume. This collection of poems told the stories of marginal people in an everyday **vernacular** form. *The Ancient Mariner*'s strange (almost hallucinatory) elements – the frozen Arctic seascape, the dead men steering the ship, the Mariner biting his own arm until it pours blood in order to quench his thirst, the murder of the albatross – can be compared with the **gothic** motifs of *Frankenstein*. The ballad form and theme of John Keats's *La Belle Dame Sans Merci* adds another dimension to Coleridge's tale of a Romantic wanderer driven to (and perhaps beyond) the point of madness, trying to make sense of his own spiritual pilgrimage, exile and home-coming as he narrates his story to the trapped Wedding Guest. If you read the poem, you will find several other contextual links to investigate.

CONCLUSION

In this chapter you have investigated some of the links between a group of writers by applying various ideas about context. Writers have often come together in groups or networks which have formed some kind of artistic nucleus, but in looking for similarities and differences, and in attempting to reference, label and classify groups, we risk distorting and oversimplifying their aims and ideas. Labels attached to texts encourage readers to look for similarities between them, and usually they can be found. But we must be alert to possible differences. Parcelling up texts into convenient categories can be too easy; problems and inconsistencies can make us reinvestigate and refine our ideas. Go back to the questions posed at the beginning of this chapter about how and why texts can be categorised. Has labelling the texts in this section helped you get to grips with them by providing a useful map of an unfamiliar literary landscape, or hindered you from making meanings of your own by encouraging you to look for specifically 'Romantic' things? The wrong type of labelling can be like examining a crime scene to prove the guilt of a particular suspect; making the evidence fit preconceived notions of guilt instead of under-taking an open investigation.

Rule-breakers, such as punks and goths, help mainstream society define itself, and, in turn, outcast groups map out their own counter-cultural space. Choosing to identify with a particular subculture allows people simultaneously to belong and not belong, and maybe this is the best of both worlds. Yet identifying with others is not always easy; the relationship between first-generation Romantics, such as Wordsworth and Coleridge, and younger colleagues, such as Byron and Shelley, was highly problematic, and Jane Austen actively sought to distance herself from what she saw as self-indulgence rather than self-actualisation. All this suggests that although writers are products of the general social context in which they operate, their work does not simply mirror the times in which they live. Moreover, readers respond in different ways to the same events and climates of opinion; this is why a search for the meaning of a text is pointless, since multiple meanings are inevitable. Both literary and non-literary texts reflect (and often pre-date) aspects of the social, cultural and historical environment in which they were produced, and readers' expectations of texts are often based on their pre-existing knowledge of an author's occupation of this working space.

SUMMARY

This chapter has done the following:

- Examined some ideas about how and why texts are labelled and organised
- Looked at how and why writers may be grouped together
- Looked at some problems that can emerge when writers are linked
- Looked at some contexts that can be applied to linked texts

SOURCES AND ADAPTATIONS   CHAPTER 4

So far in this book, readers' rather than writers' choices have triggered the comparisons you have studied. Most writers do not set out with any notion of their work being aligned with other texts in order to be compared and contrasted (sometimes very arbitrarily) by future readers. In certain distinctive cases, however, the concept of comparison is inbuilt from the start. This chapter focuses on these reworkings of **source** texts.

PARODY

The following text was never designed to be recorded permanently. Although it is written rather than spoken, it is nevertheless **ephemeral**. It is an example of an anonymous junk email, and the original context of reception for most readers would have been via their personal computer in the workplace. Few people who receive these documents even save them, let alone print them out. The usual pattern of distribution and readership for this kind of text is that it is written in response to a specific topical news story and passed on quickly to successive waves of readers. Such texts have a limited shelf life and are soon replaced, and for this reason, the original context of production needs restating. In September 2002, a mild earth tremor was felt in Dudley, near Birmingham. This **parody** spoofs the kind of charity appeal made after major natural disasters, such as floods, hurricanes and earthquakes, in foreign countries.

Exercise 1 – The Dudley Earthquake Appeal
- Analyse the form, structure and language of this transformed text and explain how the parody works.
- What linguistic conventions are used and what potential attitudes and values might it suggest?

Suggestions for answer follow on page 47.

Subject: APPEAL FOR THE VICTIMS OF THE DUDLEY EARTHQUAKE

At 00.54 on Monday 23 September an earthquake measuring 4.8 on the Richter scale hit Dudley, UK causing untold disruption and distress –

- Many were woken well before their giro arrived
- Several priceless collections of mementoes from the Balearics and Spanish costas were damaged
- Three areas of historic and scientifically significant litter were disturbed
- Thousands are confused and bewildered, trying to come to terms with the fact that something interesting has happened in Dudley
- Apparently, though, looting did continue as normal.

One resident, Donna-Marie Dutton, a 17 year old mother-of-three said, 'It was such a shock, little Chantal-Leanne came running into my bedroom crying. My youngest two, Tyler-Morgan and Megan-Storm slept through it all. I was still shaking when I was watching Trisha the next morning.'

The British Red Cross has so far managed to ship 4000 crates of Sunny Delight to the area to help the stricken masses. Rescue workers are still searching through the rubble and have found personal belongings such as benefit books and jewellery from Elizabeth Duke at Argos.

HOW YOU CAN HELP

- £2 buys chips, scraps and blue pop for a family of four
- £10 will take a family to Stourport for the day, where the children can play on an unspoiled canal bank among the national collection of stinging nettles
- 22p buys a biro for filling in a spurious compensation claim

PLEASE ACT NOW

Simply email us by return with your credit card details and we'll do the rest. If you prefer to donate cash, there are collection points available at your local branches of Argos, Iceland and Clinton Cards.

THANK YOU

Suggestions for Answer

The generic template behind the text is familiar, and you should have spotted several discourse features of persuasive writing. These include the use of the classic problem-solution **discourse** structure; the creation of a relationship between unknown author and reader – 'how you can help', 'please act now'; the use of clichéd emotive hyperbole – 'stricken masses', 'rescue workers still searching through the rubble' and also the sequence of logical, chronological steps involved in the tragedy and the subsequent donation process.

The parody blends the usual ingredients seen above with an array of unusual comic devices such as the **mock epic** form. **Epic** texts tell of hugely important events, but instead of describing an event of great significance, an essentially trivial news story is rendered extra-trivial (and thus comic) by the serious treatment. Another technique is the comic reversal of expectations: Dudley is presented as a nightmarish third-world disaster zone, in which looting is 'normal'. Varied and unusual **lexis**, from the **demotic** 'chips, scraps and blue pop' to the contrasting high-**register** 'spurious compensation claim', add a rich linguistic field.

While the humour in this piece is potentially offensive, those on the receiving end of this harsh **satire** of the urban working class are not the target audience. The email appears to express contempt for such people, as represented by the stereotyped teenaged single mother, Donna-Marie Dutton. The **pragmatics** of the text imply that the **narratee** does not watch *Trisha*, holiday on the Spanish 'costas', drink Sunny Delight or claim State benefits and that this way of life may therefore be freely criticised. However, another reading could suggest that it is the stereo-typers themselves, rather than the stereotyped, who are being laughed at. What do you think?

CASE STUDY: *PRIDE AND PREJUDICE* AND *BRIDGET JONES'S DIARY*

The rest of this chapter looks at one specific text that has inspired another: Helen Fielding's 1996 novel *Bridget Jones's Diary*, which echoes and reinter-prets Jane Austen's *Pride and Prejudice* (1813). To engage fully with the material in this chapter, you should really familiarise yourself with both of these texts, although the skills and points raised are, of course, relevant to all such textual pairings.

The best way to examine this sort of deliberate intertextual pair is to work with the key assessment objectives. A flexible approach should help you cover form, structure and language, multiple interpretations of text and also context. Some examination boards require you to deal with all three, but you may not have to pay equal attention to them, as they have different weightings as part of the overall jigsaw puzzle structure of the AS/A2 course. Check the exact requirements of your specification with your teacher.

Exercise 2 – Group Task on Romantic Novels

- With other students in your class, compile a list of the typical features of the romantic novel genre.
- Begin with the classic narrative structure – 'girl meets boy' – and discuss the extent to which the predictability of the genre affects the way in which these texts are read and received.
- List the possible positive and negative effects of this structure.

There are no suggestions for answer for this task.

COMPARING FORM, STRUCTURE AND LANGUAGE

Pride and Prejudice and *Bridget Jones's Diary* are both romantic novels. The time frame of each text is roughly a year, and this chronological framework underpins each heroine's journey towards the vanishing point of marriage to the hero and a conventional happy ending. The plot of *Pride and Prejudice*, once summed up as a gentleman changing his manners and a lady changing her mind, has an organic sense of right gradually asserting itself, partly due to the reader's familiarity with the Cinderella myth. The narrative's conclusion is dictated by the fairy-tale genre. The novel includes the classical pattern of three (as in three wishes, three princesses and three little pigs) with Elizabeth Bennet's series of marriage proposals – one from the ridiculous Mr Collins and two from the proud Mr Darcy. The heroine's ultimate reward is a handsome prince who saves her from embarrassing relatives, rather than the traditional dragon.

Bridget Jones's Diary follows the same simple pattern; Helen Fielding has admitted pilfering Austen's plot. Yet Austen's Elizabeth Bennet is not presented as actively searching for a partner like Bridget; in fact, at times she doubts that she will ever find a man with whom she can be happy. Blundering Bridget only understands that Mark Darcy is in love with her at the end of the novel, unlike Elizabeth, who is aware of Fitzwilliam Darcy's feelings for her much sooner. Readers familiar with romantic fiction in general (and *Pride and Prejudice* in particular) spot Bridget's 'Mr Right' well before she herself does. Despite many misunderstandings, Bridget and Mark move from mutual dislike to a conventional happy ending. The fact that they do not marry at the end of the book allows Helen Fielding to recycle the plot of Austen's *Persuasion* (in which the hero and heroine split up before being reunited) in her Bridget Jones sequel *The Edge of Reason*. It is therefore just as crucial for Fielding not to marry off Bridget and Mark as it was for Austen to formally consolidate the relationship of Elizabeth and Darcy.

Interestingly, *Pride and Prejudice* is itself an adaptation of an earlier 1790s source text called *First Impressions*. The novel contains so many letters and references to letters that some critics think that in her original draft version Austen might have experimented with an **epistolary** technique, which had fallen out of fashion by the time *Pride and Prejudice* was finally published. Epistolary novels are written in the form of letters, journals or diaries, sometimes apparently edited by someone other than the actual author. This form allows the letter writers or diarists to reveal intimate thoughts and feelings. Helen Fielding is also a fan of this form, describing it as

> very direct and intimate. Because it's an imaginary character, you can hide behind a persona. It also allows you to write the sort of shameful thoughts that everyone has but no one wants to admit to, since you're not trying to make anyone like you. A diary is an outlet for your most private thoughts, a very personal way of writing. And that feeling of peeping behind a curtain at someone else's life is good for a reader.

Exercise 3 – Analysing *Pride and Prejudice*

Read the following extracts from *Pride and Prejudice* and analyse Jane Austen's presentation of the feelings of Darcy and Elizabeth. Suggestions for answer follow on page 151.

This is the opening of a long letter written by Mr Darcy to Elizabeth after she has rejected his first marriage proposal. The letter confirms that Mr Darcy did interfere in his friend Mr Bingley's love affair with Elizabeth's sister Jane, wrongly believing that Jane was not very attached to Bingley. Much more shocking is Darcy's assertion that the popular and handsome George Wickham is a callous seducer who had plotted to run off with Darcy's 15-year-old sister in order to gain control of her fortune.

> Be not alarmed, Madam, on receiving this letter, by the apprehension of its containing any repetition of those sentiments, or renewal of those offers, which were last night so disgusting to you. I write without any intention of paining you, or humbling myself, by dwelling on wishes, which, for the happiness of both, cannot be too soon forgotten; and the effort which the formation, and the perusal of this letter must occasion, should have been spared, had not my character required it to be written and read. You must, therefore, pardon the freedom with which I demand your attention; your feelings, I know, will bestow it unwillingly, but I demand it of your justice.

The letter concludes (and the chapter closes):

> For the truth of every thing here related, I can appeal more particularly to the testimony of Colonel Fitzwilliam, who from our near relationship and constant intimacy, and still more as one of the executors of my father's will, has been unavoidably acquainted with every particular of these transactions. If your

continued

abhorrence of me should make my assertions valueless, you cannot be prevented by the same cause from confiding in my cousin; and that there may be the possibility of consulting him, I shall endeavour to find some opportunity of putting this letter in your hands in the course of the morning. I will only add, God bless you.

Fitzwilliam Darcy

The next chapter begins with a description of Elizabeth's feelings after reading the letter.

If Elizabeth, when Mr Darcy gave her the letter, did not expect it to contain a renewal of his offers, she had formed no expectation at all of its contents. But such as they were, it may well be supposed how eagerly she went through them, and what a contrariety of emotion they excited. Her feelings as she read were scarcely to be defined. With amazement did she first understand that he believed any apology to be in his power; and steadfastly was she persuaded that he could have no explanation to give, which a just sense of shame would not conceal. With a strong prejudice against every thing he might say, she began his account of what had happened at Netherfield. She read, with an eagerness which hardly left her power of comprehension, and from impatience of knowing what the next sentence might bring, was incapable of attending to the sense of the one before her eyes. His belief of her sister's insensibility, she instantly resolved to be false, and his account of the real, the worst objections to the match, made her too angry to have any wish of doing him justice. He expressed no regret for what he has done which satisfied her; his style was not penitent, but haughty. It was all pride and insolence.

But when this subject was succeeded by his account of Mr Wickham, when she read with clearer attention, a relation of events, which, if true, must overthrow every cherished opinion of his worth . . . her feelings were yet more acutely painful and more difficult of definition. Astonishment, apprehension, and even horror, oppressed her. She wished to discredit it entirely, repeatedly exclaiming, 'This must be false! This cannot be! This must be the grossest falsehood!' – and when she had gone through the whole letter . . . put it hastily away, protesting that she would not regard it, that she would never look in it again.

In time, Elizabeth reviews what she knows of both Wickham and Darcy, and admits the truth.

She grew absolutely ashamed of herself. Of neither Darcy nor Wickham could she think, without feeling that she had been blind, partial, prejudiced, absurd.

'How despicably have I acted!' she cried. 'I, who have prided myself on my discernment! I, who have valued myself on my abilities! who have often disdained the generous candour of my sister, and gratified my vanity, in useless or blameable distrust. How humiliating is this discovery! Yet, how just a humiliation! Had I been in love, I could not have been more wretchedly blind. But vanity, not love, has been my folly. Pleased with the preference of one, and offended by the neglect of the other, on the very beginning of our acquaintance, I have courted prepossession and ignorance, and driven reason away, where either were concerned. Till this moment, I never knew myself.'

. . . When she came to that part of the letter in which her family were mentioned, in terms of such mortifying, yet merited reproach, her sense of shame was severe. The justice of the charge struck her too forcibly for denial.

Suggestions for Answer

Throughout the novel Mr Darcy is presented dually. At first, the reader tends to accept the general view of him, but his character is redefined gradually in the light of new material revealed by Austen to Elizabeth Bennet within the text and to the reader outside it. In the context of the previous chapter on Romanticism, Mr Darcy may be seen as a Byronic hero, passionate and handsome, yet isolated and misunderstood; he is, however, rescued from his isolation by the intervention of Elizabeth Bennet.

In these extracts, Darcy argues the case for his own defence. He tries to reposition himself in Elizabeth's eyes, and this also affects the readers who have so far seen him mainly from her point of view. This narrative structure places Elizabeth in the position of an appeal court judge, comparing texts herself, in a sense. She undertakes a process of moral and emotional realignment as she indexes and cross-references Darcy's new evidence against previous statements made by George Wickham. The lexical field of the law is noticeable in both Darcy's letter and Elizabeth's response; he demands that she reads his letter 'of her justice' and urges her to refer to the 'testimony' of his cousin, 'executor' of his father's 'will'. Elizabeth prides herself on her good judgement (and admits the 'justice of the charge' when Darcy makes a counter-claim against her family.) Austen's first person narrative (Darcy's entire letter is in speech marks) creates the sense of a dialogue between the two characters. Elizabeth makes several agitated spoken outbursts as she responds to Darcy's argument. The dense texture of the prose, its long sentences studded with a variety of punctuation marks reflecting pauses of varying lengths – commas, semicolons, colons and dashes – mimics the shifting emotions of both characters.

Exercise 4 – Comparing Form, Structure and Language

The following extract from *Bridget Jones's Diary* refers to the BBC television version of *Pride and Prejudice*. Compare and contrast the ways in which Helen Fielding and Jane Austen use form, structure and language to present their heroines. Suggestions for answer are at the back of the book.

> Sunday 15 October
>
> 9st (better), alcohol units 5 (but special occasion), cigarettes 16, calories 2456, minutes spent thinking about Mr Darcy 245.
>
> 8.55a.m. Just nipped out for fags prior to getting changed ready for BBC Pride and Prejudice. Hard to believe there are so many cars out on the roads. Shouldn't they be at home getting ready? Love the nation being so addicted. The basis of my own addiction, I know, is my simple human need for Darcy to get off with Elizabeth. Tom says football guru Nick Hornby says in his book that men's obsession with football is not vicarious. The testosterone-crazed fans do not wish themselves on the pitch, claims Hornby, instead seeing their team as their chosen representatives, rather like parliament. That is precisely my feeling about Darcy and Elizabeth. They are my chosen representatives in the field of shagging, or, rather, courtship. I do not, however, wish to see any actual goals. I would hate to see Darcy and Elizabeth in bed, smoking a cigarette afterwards. That would be unnatural and wrong and I would quickly lose interest.
>
> 10.30 a.m. Jude just called and we spent twenty minutes growling, 'Fawaw, that Mr Darcy.' I love the way he talks, sort of as if he can't be bothered. Ding-dong! Then we has a long discussion about the comparative merits of Mr Darcy and Mark Darcy, both agreeing that Mr Darcy was more attractive because he was ruder but that being imaginary was a disadvantage that could not be overlooked.

INTERPRETATIONS OF TEXTS

One of the best-known interpretations of *Pride and Prejudice* is the 1995 BBC television adaptation written by Andrew Davies, who also collaborated with Helen Fielding on the 2001 film version of *Bridget Jones's Diary*. In the film version, Renée Zellweger's Bridget paraphrases the famous opening line of *Pride and Prejudice* in voice-over, stating, 'It is a truth universally acknowledged that the moment one area of your life starts going OK, another part of it falls spectacularly to pieces.' After the film's release, Fielding's ironic textual references to the television version of *Pride and Prejudice* (let alone the episode in the sequel *The Edge of Reason* when Bridget actually interviews the actor Colin Firth) invite the reader to revise their original response to the written text. Now that the same Colin Firth who was Jane Austen's Mr Darcy on the small screen has played Helen

Fielding's Mark Darcy on the big screen, the boundary between Colin Firth as a minor character mentioned in Fielding's text and Colin Firth as a successful actor is blurred. You might also consider the extent to which Colin Firth was playing Andrew Davies's versions of the two Mr Darcys.

Andrew Davies's adaptations of *Pride and Prejudice* and *Bridget Jones's Diary* may now work as intertextual companion pieces: there must be far more people who have read his modern versions than either of the original novels. When the BBC ran its *Big Read* series in the winter of 2003, Davies argued the case for *Pride and Prejudice* as the nation's favourite book. The huge popularity of his television adaptation has apparently authorised him to represent Jane Austen for mass consumption. Is Andrew Davies's Jane Austen now the state-sponsored, officially sanctioned version?

THE WRITER'S CONTEXT

No writer's work can be divorced from the circumstances of their life and times, and researching the backgrounds of Jane Austen and Helen Fielding in your college library or on the Internet would show you that whereas Jane Austen stayed in the countryside writing in secret, Helen Fielding went to Oxford University and worked at the BBC, earning fame and success. Another contrast is the temporal space occupied by each text. It is possible to date the events of Fielding's novel exactly, as it records the precise Sunday dates in the autumn of 1995 when the BBC version of *Pride and Prejudice* was originally broadcast. Third, although soldiers cause havoc in *Pride and Prejudice*, Jane Austen resolutely declines to engage with the issues of war despite her contemporaries' obsession with the fear of Napoleon Bonaparte and what the French army might do next.

Just as Helen Fielding has been seen as capturing the **zeitgeist** of late post-feminism in the 1990s, so Austen's text has been interpreted as a debate about the key intellectual and cultural movements of her age, the Enlightenment and Romanticism. Some critics have seen Darcy and Elizabeth as emblems of these two ideologies; his rational Enlightenment virtues offset her Romantic energy to create a harmonious equilibrium. While it is possible to see Mr Darcy as the archetypal Romantic hero – albeit one who is also seen to possess the Enlightenment virtues of good judgement, taste and a well-governed temper – it is usually Elizabeth who is seen as the Romantic rebel.

THE TEXT'S CONTEXT

In her lifetime, Jane Austen defended and concealed her position as a writer. Her books were published anonymously, the title pages stating only that the author was 'a Lady', and her brother Henry dealt with the business side of her career. This context of production and reception is important: Helen Fielding has been attacked for inventing the genre of 'chick-lit', which some critics have seen as patronising to women, yet Jane Austen also had to resist the denunciation of her chosen genre. In the late eighteenth and early nineteenth century, while most novelists and novel readers were women, most reviewers and critics were men. This doubly female genre was condemned by writers such as Samuel Taylor Coleridge, who stated that 'where the reading of novels prevails as a habit, it occasions in time the entire destruction of the power of the mind'. If you have ever been told that watching too much television will rot your brain, you may sympathise with Austen's robust fight back; a section of her early book *Northanger Abbey* is now known as her 'Defence of the Novel'. These critical views and perspectives may affect the way modern readers receive *Pride and Prejudice*.

Another contextual factor is the fact that both texts were originally produced in formats dependent on frequent narrative climaxes. *Pride and Prejudice* was first published in three volumes, so Austen built in cliff-hanger endings at the end of each book to persuade the reader to purchase the next one. Therefore in Volume I mistakes are made and prejudices formed, Volume II sees both plot and relationships become more complex, and Volume III draws everything to a harmonious conclusion. Similarly, *Bridget Jones's Diary* first appeared in weekly instalments in a national newspaper, the *Independent*. As a columnist, Fielding had to create a feeling of familiarity and continuity for her regular readers, while also making each episode self-contained and understandable by new readers.

THE READER'S CONTEXT

Just as Jane Austen was a product of her age, so you are a product of yours. How you respond to these texts about the privileged, white, upper-middle classes of 200 years ago will depend on your own experiences, ideas and values.

During the BBC's 2003 *Big Read* series, actor and writer Meera Syal presented a short film on *Pride and Prejudice*, in which she linked the novel's emphasis on marriage as 'a deal done between families' with her own British-Asian culture: 'in some strange way,' she commented, 'I felt this book was about me'. Syal stressed the modernity of Austen's concerns and invited the television viewers to respond in the same way: 'take away the bonnets and the ballgowns and this timeless romance could be happening in your office or my street'. She argued that *Pride and Prejudice* contains 'the DNA of all romantic comedies. . . . It is the smartest, funniest book ever written about the battle of the sexes'. Austen's trademark witty dialogue is offered as another modern aspect of the text: 'banter as foreplay – how very twenty-first century!' The way in which Austen keeps Darcy and Elizabeth apart – making 'the inevitable seem impossible' – is 'a masterclass in delayed gratification'. *Pride and Prejudice* is 'a fairytale with attitude', which 'will always travel across continents and centuries because its appeal is timeless'.

Consider the extent to which *Pride and Prejudice*'s special status affects your personal response to the text. Can you separate the text itself from the cultural baggage attached to it as supposedly England's most popular classic novel?

Clearly, *Bridget Jones's Diary* is not expected to bear the weight of expectation and cultural capital attached to *Pride and Prejudice*. It is much more likely that many readers see it simply as a funny book – no more and no less. But with your wider understanding of the novel and its intertextual links with Austen's text, do you still read it in this way? Is there a sense in which problematising and complicating *Bridget Jones's Diary* from a literary point of view risks spoiling your straight-forward enjoyment of it?

THE READING'S CONTEXT

Think about other theories and methods you could apply to these texts to make meanings. Different critical schools will obviously emphasise distinctive aspects of each text, or interpret the same episode in a variety of ways. For example, one of the central events of *Pride and Prejudice* is Elizabeth's visit to Darcy's country estate, Pemberley. From a moral or psychological standpoint, Pemberley may be Darcy's **objective correlative**; a symbolic representation of the man himself. Elizabeth is shown a small portrait of him (seeing him, quite literally, in miniature) at the start of her tour of his house, which can be read as an interior journey. Eventually, her quest culminates in her discovery of Darcy's full-length portrait in the gallery amid his ancestors. Regarding this 'with earnest contemplation', she feels she 'could have softened that look'. Symbolically, Elizabeth plays detective in Darcy's house, and the mystery that she solves is Darcy himself.

On the other hand, Darcy's position as a wealthy landowner and all-powerful patriarchal figure lends itself to a Marxist reinterpretation, as he rejects the dying aristocracy personified by his cousin and allies himself with the emerging bour-geoisie, symbolised by Elizabeth Bennet. To a modern audience, Darcy's role as monarch of all he surveys may well seem more sinister and parasitical than paternalistic and enlightened. Helen Fielding's human rights lawyer, Mark Darcy, has to earn his high status as a powerful man who assumes responsibility for the less fortunate, which is ironic, given that Elizabeth Bennet's uncle is sneered at for being an attorney in *Pride and Prejudice*. In a modern social and cultural context, the hero cannot be an aristocratic landowner living on unearned income, but Fitzwilliam Darcy's right to inherit vast wealth is never questioned by Jane Austen; indeed, the hierarchical and patriarchal English class structure (symbolised by Pemberley) is presented as the natural order of things. The subversive antics of the steward's son George Wickham, who tries to annex Darcy's power and influence, are severely punished.

Feminist critics of *Bridget Jones's Diary* have pointed to gaps in this apparently simple comic text where important questions go unasked. When Bridget realises that she has been on a diet for so long that 'the idea that you might actually need calories to survive has been completely wiped out of [her] consciousness', questions are raised about the negative opinion that many women have of themselves – often derived from media images of impossibly beautiful, thin models. Yet women co-operate in this process by buying the very magazines that make them feel bad about themselves. By adopting an oppositional reading position, is it possible to read *Bridget Jones's Diary* as a subversive feminist polemic?

Exercise 5 – Class Discussion

- Discuss with the other students in your class the extent to which you think is it worth reading a homage text without knowing about or researching its links with the original source text.
- What is gained or lost by reading the reworked version as an independent, stand-alone text?

There are no suggestions for answer for this exercise.

CONCLUSION

In this chapter you have compared two linked texts in order to establish the similarities and differences between them. What has emerged is far more challenging than a simple correlation of events and modernisation of the language; instead, the contexts of each book allow the reader to draw parallels between the positions of two women writers separated by almost two centuries. Other well-known source texts and adaptations include *The Coral Island* (R.M. Ballantyne) and *Lord of the Flies* (William Golding), *North and South* (Elizabeth Gaskell) and *Nice Work* (David Lodge), and *Jane Eyre* (Charlotte Brontë) and *Wide Sargasso Sea* (Jean Rhys).

SUMMARY

This chapter has done the following:

- Explored the notion of reworking a source text
- Considered the implications of deliberately interweaving new texts and old
- Examined the form, structure and language of two linked texts
- Worked through some contexts linked to the Literature Assessment Objectives

---

CHAPTER 5

COMPARING TEXTS IN EXAMINATIONS

The first four chapters of this book have explored several ways of comparing texts and this section brings all these ideas together. This chapter focuses on preparing for the kind of comparative tasks set in examinations. Comparing texts under timed conditions can be daunting, because someone else (i.e. the examiner) has chosen the texts for you, and you may worry that the key links, similarities and differences might not be clear to you (or even if there are any). In this chapter you will work through two comparative exercises in order to practise key exam skills.

If you are studying English Literature or a combined Language/Literature course, you may be comparing pre-release material that you have had two or three days to study with new material that you will see for the first time on the day of the examination. It is worth discussing in class the advantages and disadvantages of this process, in order to analyse your own working methods and strategies and learn from the ideas of others. You could revise for the synoptic unit and your set texts simultaneously, by brainstorming all the similarities and differences you can think of between them.

If you are studying English Language, you may have to sift and compare a variety of unseen texts, and one active revision method that can give you real insight into how these papers work is to write your own version. This is not as difficult as it sounds; in pairs or small groups, simply collect a variety of texts and try to categorise them.

For most students, the ultimate examination nightmare is being asked lots of questions that they cannot answer. In reality this situation is more likely to be faced by a contestant on a game show such as *The Weakest Link* than a student taking a modern A Level English exam. Luckily for you, the exam texts chosen for you to compare have been selected to enable all students to show what they know. Random connections are only for pub quizzes.

CASE STUDY 1: COMPARING LITERARY TEXTS

In the next section, you will be comparing three literary texts. One of these extracts is from the *General Prologue to the Canterbury Tales*, written in the late 1300s by

Geoffrey Chaucer, a diplomat and civil servant with connections to the royal court. The *General Prologue* introduces a motley group of pilgrims journeying to the shrine of St Thomas à Becket in Canterbury. Very few of them are genuinely religious; most are materialistic social climbers and outright villains. A competition is arranged in which the travellers will tell stories along the way to pass the time and entertain each other.

'Text' is of course the root of linked words such as '**subtext**', 'context' and 'intertextuality'. It is useful to remember that 'textile' is also part of this word family, as this draws attention to the continuous process of weaving and inter-weaving that goes on between texts. Chaucer was engaged in this process more than 600 years ago, just as you are today. He collected, translated, edited, rewrote and rearranged an assortment of myths, legends, poems and stories doing the rounds in medieval Europe, and organised them using the device of the pilgrimage. The story-telling challenge arranged by the Host of the Tabard Inn in Southwark is the frame that integrates each separate tale into the whole design – and allows for some interesting juxtapositions; for instance, the Clerk's tale of patient Griselda, an uncomplaining and passive medieval wife, is designed to invalidate and rebut the 'feminist' lecture of the Wife of Bath who precedes him.

The *General Prologue* introduces all the pilgrims, and Chaucer himself tags along as the narrator. Chaucer binds together his diverse collection of stories – romantic, tragic, funny and filthy – using a structural framework that allows him to group together characters from many social classes or medieval 'estates'. One of the most famous of all Chaucer's characters is the Wife of Bath, whose portrait follows below.

Exercise 1 – Comparing Literary Texts

In the following extracts, Geoffrey Chaucer writes about an experienced woman of the world, Jane Austen writes about the romantic problems encountered by Elizabeth Bennet and Carol Ann Duffy writes about the widowed Anne Hathaway's love for her husband, William Shakespeare.

Compare and contrast the ways in which the three writers convey their ideas about women, love and marriage. Suggestions for answer are at the back of the book.

Text A

Geoffrey Chaucer – 'The Wife of Bath' (*c.* 1390)

A good Wif was ther of biside Bathe,
But she was somdel deef, and that was scathe.
Of clooth-making she hadde swich an haunt,
She passed hem of Ypres and of Gaunt.
In all the parrisshe wif ne was ther noon

That to the offringe before hire sholde goon;
And if ther dide, certeyn so wrothe was she,
That she was out of alle charitee.
Hir coverchiefs ful fine weren of ground;
I dorste swere they weyeden ten pound
That on a Sonday weren upon hir heed.
Hir hosen weren of fyn scarlet reed,
Ful streite yteyd, and shoes ful moiste and newe.
Boold was hir face, and fair, and reed of hewe.
She was a worthy womman all hir live:
Housbands at chirche dore she hadde five,
Withouten oother compaignye in youthe, –
But therof nedeth nat to speke as nowthe.
And thries hadde she been at Jerusalem;
She had passed many a straunge strem;
At Rome she hadde been, and at Boloigne,
In Galice at Seint-Jame, and at Coloigne.
She koulde muchel of wandringe by the weye.
Gat-tothed was she, soothly for to seye.
Upon and amblere esily she sat,
Ywimpled wel, and on hir heed an hat
As brood as is a bokeler or a targe;
A foot-mantel aboute hir hipes large,
And on hir feet a paire of spores sharpe.
In felaweshipe wel koude she laughe and carpe.
Of remedies of love she knew per chaunce,
For she koude of that art the olde daunce.

The following translation will help you with the text above, but in your answer you
should write about the original version.

There was a good wife from near Bath
But she was somewhat deaf, and that was a pity.
She had such skill in cloth making
She surpassed the weavers of Ypres and Ghent.
In the entire parish there was no wife
Who should go up to the altar before her;
And if anyone did, she would certainly be so angry
That she was out of all charity.
Her headscarves were of the finest cloth;
I dare swear that her Sunday best weighed ten pounds

continued

When they were on her head.
Her stockings were of a fine scarlet red,
Very tightly stretched, with shoes of supple, soft leather.
Her face was bold, fair and red in colour.
She was a worthy woman all her life:
She had had five husbands at the church door
Not including other male company she had kept in her youth –
But there's no need to go into all that.
And she had been to Jerusalem three times;
She had crossed many a foreign river;
She had been to Rome, and Boulogne,
Santiago de Compostela in Spain, and to Cologne.
She knew all about wandering by the wayside.
To tell the truth, she was gap-toothed.
She sat easily on a comfortable old horse,
Wrapped up in a wimple, and with a hat on her head
As wide as a shield or archery target;
An overcoat around her large rump,
And a pair of sharp spurs on her feet.
In company she was always laughing and gossiping.
She probably knew all about love potions
For she understood everything about that old game.

This extract from *Pride and Prejudice* appeared in Chapter 4, so it functions here as an example of pre-release material; that is, a text issued a few days before the examination with which you have the chance to become familiar. You may wish to refer back to Chapter 4 to remind yourself of some of the novel's contexts.

Text B

Jane Austen – *Pride and Prejudice* (1813)

If Elizabeth, when Mr Darcy gave her the letter, did not expect it to contain a renewal of his offers, she had formed no expectation at all of its contents. But such as they were, it may well be supposed how eagerly she went through them, and what a contrariety of emotion they excited. Her feelings as she read were scarcely to be defined. With amazement did she first understand that he believed any apology to be in his power; and steadfastly was she persuaded that he could have no explanation to give, which a just sense of shame would not conceal. With a strong prejudice against every thing he might say, she began his account of what had happened at Netherfield. She read, with an eagerness which hardly left her power of comprehension, and from impatience of knowing what the next sentence might bring, was incapable of attending to the sense of the one before her eyes. His belief of her sister's insensibility, she instantly resolved to be false, and his account of the real, the worst objections to the match, made her too angry to have any wish of doing him justice. He expressed no regret for what he has done which satisfied her; his style was not penitent, but haughty. It was all pride and insolence.

But when this subject was succeeded by his account of Mr Wickham, when she read with clearer attention, a relation of events, which, if true, must overthrow every cherished opinion of his worth. her feelings were yet more acutely painful and more difficult of definition. Astonishment, apprehension, and even horror, oppressed her. She wished to discredit it entirely, repeatedly exclaiming, 'This must be false! This cannot be! This must be the grossest falsehood!' – and when she had gone through the whole letter . . . put it hastily away, protesting that she would not regard it, that she would never look in it again.

. . . She grew absolutely ashamed of herself. Of neither Darcy nor Wickham could she think, without feeling that she had been blind, partial, prejudiced, absurd.

'How despicably have I acted!' she cried. 'I, who have prided myself on my discernment! I, who have valued myself on my abilities! who have often disdained the generous candour of my sister, and gratified my vanity, in useless or blameable distrust. How humiliating is this discovery! Yet, how just a humiliation! Had I been in love, I could not have been more wretchedly blind. But vanity, not love, has been my folly. Pleased with the preference of one, and offended by the neglect of the other, on the very beginning of our acquaintance, I have courted prepossession and ignorance, and driven reason away, where either were concerned. Till this moment, I never knew myself.'

Text C is taken from a collection of poems called *The World's Wife*, in which Carol Ann Duffy makes use of myths, legends, Bible tales and history to reinterpret traditional stories. The collection alters and subverts conventional narratives by giving a voice to marginalised and excluded female characters, such as Queen Kong, Elvis's Twin Sister and Frau Freud. Duffy prefaces this poem about Shakespeare's widow, Anne Hathaway, with an extract from the playwright's will, which has usually been read as revealing his dislike for her.

Text C

Carol Ann Duffy – 'Anne Hathaway' (1999)

'Item I gyve unto my wife my second best bed . . .'
(from Shakespeare's will)

The bed we loved in was a spinning world
of forests, castles, torchlights, clifftops, seas
where he would dive for pearls. My lover's words
were shooting stars which fell to earth as kisses
on these lips; my body now a softer rhyme
to his, now echo, assonance; his touch
a verb dancing in the centre of a noun.
Some nights, I dreamed he'd written me, the bed
a page beneath his writer's hands. Romance
and drama played by touch, by scent, by taste.
In the other bed, the best, our guests dozed on,
dribbling their prose. My living laughing love –

CASE STUDY 2: COMPARING NON-LITERARY TEXTS

In the next section you will be comparing non-literary texts of various types. One text in the following group appeared in Chapter 3, and has been reprinted to remind you of the notion of intertextuality. If one of the texts on your exam paper seems to have strong links with another text you have come across, it may well be appropriate to refer to it.

Exercise 2: Comparing Non-Literary Texts

Read Texts A–E, which illustrate different varieties of language use. One you have seen before; the others are new. Compare and contrast the language features of the texts and explain how these may be affected by context. Use some of these language frameworks where appropriate:

* Lexis
* Grammar
* Phonology
* Semantics
* Discourse
* Pragmatics
* Graphology

Suggestions for answer are at the back of the book.

The following transcript (Text A) is part of a conversation between Lydia (13) and her mother Jane, a teacher, about the day's events at school.

Words between vertical lines are spoken simultaneously, underlining indicates emphasis in speech and (.) indicates a brief pause.

Text A

JANE: so did anything much happen today is Abby still poorly did you have um French did you get your mark for the um exam um test back or

LYDIA: Abby was off <u>again</u> and she hadn't marked it /but/

JANE: /but/ you did it last week didn't you I mean it <u>was</u> /last/

LYDIA: /mum/ honestly it was only a pathetic <u>test</u> and it was for like <u>six year</u> <u>olds</u> just don't bother

JANE: OK fine yes well anyway OK so what <u>did</u> happen

LYDIA: well you know John

JANE: um John with the hair or um funny John

LYDIA: funny John John with the hair is going out with Sophie

JANE: is he Sophie Taylor I saw her mum in Next last Saturday

LYDIA: no Sophie <u>Simpson</u> cos Sophie Taylor's in Year 10 (.) <u>anyway</u>

JANE: OK right yes so yes funny John and

LYDIA: well funny John well he sort of (.) well we were sort of stood outside and

JANE: standing yes

LYDIA: <u>Mum god</u> well are you listening or

JANE: yes yes I am so funny John yes funny John

LYDIA: yes well he sort of asked you know if I would go out with him and

JANE: did he ah

LYDIA: but I mean I had to say (.) well I couldn't say yes could I I um I mean well (.)

JANE: because (.)

LYDIA: Mum Emily only dumped him last week and (.)

JANE: yes but if <u>she</u> dumped <u>him</u>

LYDIA: yes but it's like a you know well it's a reboundy thing isn't it (.) isn't it (.) it's obvious

JANE: not necessarily no he's a nice boy I think he must just like you

LYDIA: well anyway (.) well I said no /but/

JANE: /well/ maybe you know you might change your mind

Text B is an extract from an A Level Communication Studies textbook, which appeared in Chapter 3.

Text B

Each of us inevitably belongs to a variety of groups.

You could list those groups you joined from your own choice, for example, a youth club or a pop group. You could also list those groups you joined without a free choice, for example, your family or your school. There are many different sorts of groups with different sorts of purposes. They cater for our different needs. These needs may be short-term (an evening party) or long-term (a club that we belong to). It is interesting to consider why we join and form various groupings.

The word 'group' can carry many different meanings and associations.

It is helpful to describe different types of groups according to their functions and qualities. We have just noted that some are short-lived gatherings of people and others are more permanent gatherings. Some are formal, others informal. Some are small (say, five people), others are large (say, several hundred). Some are local, others international. People in a group have some interest or purpose in common which brings them together.

Although **individuals in a group share common interests**, these people may not always share all of themselves. Having agreed on some purposes, people may disagree fiercely about how these purposes should be achieved. They might disagree on how the group should be organised. Some members may want all members to be equal, but other members may prefer to have a designated leader for others to follow. When people gather together there is usually some sort of struggle for power.

Relationships and patterns of communication have to be developed for the group to function. **If there is no interaction between the individuals, then a group cannot be formed.**

Text C is an extract from Nora Ephron's account of writing the screenplay for the 1989 romantic comedy *When Harry Met Sally.*

Text C

Here is what I always say about screenwriting. When you write a script, it's like delivering a great big beautiful plain pizza, the one with only cheese and tomatoes. And then you give it to the director, and the director says; 'I love this pizza. I am willing to commit to this pizza. But I really think this pizza should have mushrooms on it.' And you say: 'Mushrooms! Of course! I meant to put mushrooms on the pizza! Why didn't I think of that? Let's put some on immediately.' And then someone else comes along and says: 'I love this pizza too, but it really needs green peppers.' 'Great,' you say. 'Green peppers. Just the thing.' And then someone else says: 'Anchovies.' There's always a fight over the anchovies. And when you get done, what you have is a pizza with everything. Sometimes it's wonderful. And sometimes you look at it and you think, I knew we shouldn't have put the green peppers on it. Why didn't I say so at the time?

. . . When a movie like *When Harry Met Sally* opens, people come to ask you questions about it. And for a few brief weeks, you become an expert. You give the impression that you knew what you were doing all along. You become an expert on the possibilities of love, on the differences between men and women. But the truth is that when you work on a movie, you don't sit around thinking: we're making a movie about the difference between men and women. You just do it. You say, this scene works for me, but this one doesn't. You say, this is good, but this could be funnier.

Text D appears to be an article from a 1950s magazine called *Housekeeping Monthly*, offering advice to married women. In fact, there was no such magazine and the article is a spoof document, which has been published on the Internet.

Text D

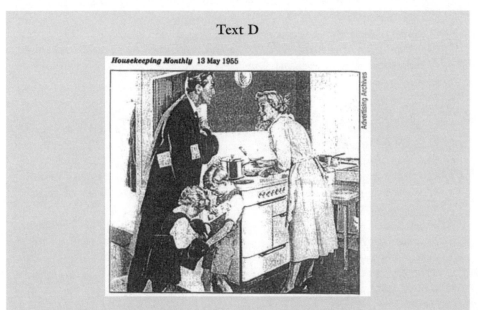

Housekeeping Monthly 13 May 1955

- Have dinner ready. Plan ahead, even the night before, to have a delicious meal ready on time for his return. This is a way of

continued

letting him know that you have been thinking about him and are concerned for his needs. Most men are hungry when they get home and the prospect of a good meal is part of the warm welcome needed.

- Prepare yourself. Take fifteen minutes to rest so you'll be refreshed when he arrives. Touch up your make-up, put a ribbon in your hair and be fresh-looking. He has just been with a lot of work-weary people.
- Be a little gay and a little more interesting for him. His boring day may need a lift and one of your duties is to provide it.
- Clear away the clutter. Make one last trip through the main part of the house just before your husband arrives. Run a dust cloth over the tables.
- During the cooler months of the year you should prepare and light a fire for him to unwind by. Your husband will feel he has reached a haven of peace and order and it will give you a lift too.
- Minimise all noise. At the time of his arrival, eliminate all noise of the washer, dryer or vacuum.
- Prepare the children. Take a minute to wash the children's hands and faces (if they are small), comb their hair and, if necessary, change their clothes. They are little treasures and he would like to see them playing the part.
- Be happy to see him.
- Greet him with a warm smile and show sincerity in your desire to please him.
- Listen to him. You may have a dozen important things to tell him, but the moment of his arrival is not the time. Let him talk first – remember his topics of conversation are more important than yours.
- Don't greet him with complaints and problems.
- Don't complain if he's late for dinner or even if he stays out all night. Count this as minor compared to what he might have gone through at work.
- Make him comfortable. Have him lean back in a comfortable chair or lie down in the bedroom. Have a cool or warm drink ready for him.
- Arrange his pillow and offer to take off his shoes. Speak in a low, soothing and pleasant voice.
- Don't ask him questions about his actions or question his judgment or integrity. Remember, he is the master of the house and as such will always exercise his will with fairness and truthfulness. You have no right to question him.
- A good wife always knows her place.

Text E comprises several comments posted on an Internet message board called Very Opinionated.com in response to *The Good Wife's Guide* (Text D). All messages are printed exactly as they originally appeared.

Text E

I'm 22 years old and I am a married women. I agree with this Good Wifes Guide. I am happy with my life and being a homemaker. I feel sorry for you women that feel that this is a load of crap. Oh also 'Some of you might be thinking that 'It must be nice that you can afford to stay home' Truth is not really but, my husband wants me to stay home. I am perfectly fine with that. A good wife is to be loving and submissive to her husband. You all think that I'm crazy, but my home is much happier this way. Read Proverbs 31 if you have the chance.

Mari

bleh bleh POOP!

Innocent Bystander

I found it highly amusing. If you cook somebody the same 'favourite' dish every night, I'd imagine he'd be pretty fed up of it after a while. Children are not little treasures, they are crusty snot covered little sods. And as for men's conversations being more important of course this was the case at the time. If women were spending all day in the home, what little titbits of interest could they provide? No hilarious stories of one's best bud photocopying his fat rear end, no savage injuries involving over-loaded staplers. They may be able to tell you what happened in Neighbours I suppose.

Joe

It's satire, people.

Ary

Highest standard of living in the world . . . ever.
Yet these women always find something to complain about.
My platoon sergeant said it best 'Stupid people seldom feel they are stupid.'
Is it any wonder western men are discarding western women by the score in favour of eastern european women?

Glenn

continued

CONCLUSION: COMPARING TEXTS IN EXAMINATIONS – METHODS AND APPROACHES

The final section of this chapter contains strategies and advice designed to help you gain high marks in your final exams. Obviously this book is a guide rather than a manual, and only you can take responsibility for what you think and write, but examiners are often surprised by students who fail to do themselves justice not through a lack of understanding, but due to poor exam technique. As you read through these suggestions, see which of them apply to you, and think about ways in which you could use some of them. You could discuss a few of the ideas with other students in your class – and see if your teacher recognises them as faults that he or she has noticed in the group's practice examination answers.

- *Work with the Assessment Objectives.* These are usually printed on the exam paper to remind you of the focus of each question. Stick to them carefully.
- *Answer the question.* Your teachers will tell you to answer the exact question set rather than twisting it to fit your own agenda – and they are right, of course. But this does not mean that you must try to read the examiner's mind and fathom one magic right answer by osmosis or intuition. There will be several ways of approaching any given question and examiners never assume that there is just one built-in answer. The real right answer is carefully structured, clearly argued, relevant and interesting. While there will be a central core of knowledge you are expected to discuss, English questions are open rather than closed, and your personal opinion matters.
- *Range around the texts.* It may seem logical to trace links between texts chrono-logically, but avoid adopting a 'listy' approach. There is no need to mention every link you find just because it is there. Examiners sometimes face woolly answers in which students have peppered their papers with every random thought that they have ever had about the texts. You cannot include everything, and it is better to write in detail on fewer points than to rush through a breathless tick list. Work out what you want to say, plan your ideas, argue your case and stop.
- *Do not swallow the thesaurus.* Use technical jargon only when it clarifies your argument. You must understand all the literary and/or linguistic terminology you use and make sure your reader can follow your argument. Unless you can explain and analyse a point in detail, merely name-checking a technical term is

useless. It is much better to work out a thoughtful and jargon-free response than to construct a fluent but empty answer to which the examiner's reaction will be either 'and?' or 'so what?'

- *Quote smart.* Include carefully chosen short references; copying out vast chunks of text is a waste of precious exam time and draws attention to your inability to select the right word or line to clinch your argument. Incorporate brief quotations into the fabric of your own writing to make your point effectively.
- *Sustain the idea of a debate.* Refer to possibilities rather than certainties. Modal verbs convey an awareness of unfixed meanings, so sentences that include phrases such as 'may be seen as', 'might be interpreted as' or 'could be represented as' will suggest alertness to the possibilities and potentialities in texts. In English Language papers, always relate texts to context, and in English Literature link your points about the structure of the text to an awareness of a variety of multiple readings and interpretations.
- *Be organised but flexible.* A few lucky students can keep an essay plan in their head, spell perfectly and quote from memory. Most can not. A good idea is to write less and plan, draft and proofread more. Be adaptable, however; if something new strikes you while you are writing, change the structure of your answer to include it.
- *Think broadly.* This book has constantly emphasised the concept of intertextuality – and so should you. The texts on your exam paper – whether literary or non-literary – will interconnect with other academic subjects you are studying as well as with wider aspects of the world around you. Be open-minded, flexible and adventurous with regard to your range of references. If you can see an interesting link between an exam text and another text, be it poem, play, novel, film, soap opera, sitcom, advertisement or pop song, go ahead and compare them. If you feel your comparison is relevant, trust your instincts. Marks are not deducted for doing something different, even if it does not quite work. Most examiners will thank you for trying.
- *Finish in style.* End your answer with a crisp conclusion that sums up your personal opinion: you could state which text interests you most and give reasons for your choice. Your conclusion is a great chance to clinch your argument and leave the examiner with a positive final impression.

Exercise 6 – The DIY Exam Kit

This final task should be done in pairs or small groups.

- Find three or four (both literary and non-literary) texts of your own which can be compared with some of the new texts in this chapter.
- Give copies of these texts to other students in your class and see how they get on. They should, in turn, provide you with an opportunity to do the same.

There are no suggestions for answer for this exercise; instead you should provide these in order to help your fellow students complete the task you have set. Good Luck!

SUMMARY

This chapter has done the following:

- Encouraged you to audit your own progress in comparing literary and non-literary texts under examination conditions
- Provided two exam questions for you to work through with suggestions for answer
- Looked at ways in which you can improve your exam technique

SUGGESTIONS FOR ANSWER

CHAPTER 1, EXERCISE 2

Nigella Lawson's Key Lime Pie Recipe

The following discourse features of instructional writing are to be found in the text:

- Title of product – '(Key) Lime Pie'
- Detailed description of end result – 'a really green pie is a dyed pie'
- Possible explanation/justification for use of unusual ingredient – 'Don't be put off by the condensed milk'
- List of required ingredients and equipment – 'For the filling' . . . 'For the base'
- Logical, chronological sequence of steps involved and use of temporal connectives – 'when', 'then', 'before', 'until', 'while'
- Imperative verb forms used to direct the task – 'preheat', 'blitz', 'press'
- Factual and informative style – 'You need an electric mixer for this'

CHAPTER 1, EXERCISE 5

Anthony Bourdain

Like Nora Ephron, Bourdain is not only an American, but also more specifically a New Yorker; his macho style, however, is very different from the black humour of Ephron's fictional character Delia. Perhaps you linked his authoritative, crisp and forthright voice with that of Elizabeth David; neither of them can be said to have a verbose or over-decorated style. You might even have compared Bourdain's confident and individual personal viewpoint with that of Nigella Lawson.

CHAPTER 3, EXERCISE 4

The Romantics

It is easy to see the apparent similarities between these texts, especially in terms of subject matter. Byron and Shelley share a political context, and Wordsworth's poem is also set against the background of the Napoleonic wars. In his poem, Wordsworth depicts a character who blends into the landscape so completely that the birds do not even notice him; an isolated human figure in harmony with the natural world. The old man is a remote figure, apparently enjoying his solitude and privacy – yet his wandering is not aimless, and he has a fixed goal in sight. The vanishing point of his journey is the bedside of his dying son in Falmouth; a family tragedy seems inevitable, and perhaps our only doubt is whether the father or the son will die first. The war in which the soldier has been injured was triggered by the revolution in France and the rise of Napoleon; these 'little people' have become enmeshed in the policies and decisions taken by powerful men they have never met. The first-generation Romantic poets – Wordsworth, Blake and Coleridge – were passionate supporters of the French Revolution, and the second-wave poets – Byron, Keats and especially Shelley – were equally enthusiastic at first. If *Ozymandias* is seen in a political context, the tyrant may represent Napoleon Bonaparte. In this sonnet, published just after Napoleon's final defeat at Waterloo, the wandering stranger conveys a stark message about the rule of any tyrant with delusions of absolute, permanent power.

In *Sense and Sensibility*, Jane Austen uses the iconic figure of the Romantic hero to open up a comic gap between fantasy and everyday life. The narrator describes the mysterious Mr Willoughby in apparently very positive terms. He is 'uncommonly handsome', 'graceful' and possesses 'youth, beauty and elegance'. The praise intensifies and the interest and admiration of the whole Dashwood family is made clear. Yet the description of Willoughby presents his 'exterior attractions' only, and opens up a potential gap between the surface and the substance of the man. In the third paragraph, the narrative moves away from the family's response to focus on Marianne's point of view. While Marianne casts Willoughby as her story-book hero, the narrator invites the reader to question her opinion. The shakiness of her judgement is revealed. When Marianne judges Willoughby by his looks, house and clothing, we are alerted to the possibility of future discrepancies between appearance and reality.

In *Frankenstein*, as the monster reads 'Paradise Lost' he contextualises his own alienation by referring to the creation of Adam. He sees that both of them are not born but created – but that Adam was loved and protected by God and given Eve as his companion. His father, on the other hand, abandons the monster, and the creature comes to equate himself with Satan. Mary Shelley's presentation of the monster questions the fixed concepts of good and evil, and the influence of nature and nurture on the development of humankind. The monster's isolation is not presented as the voluntary solitude of Wordsworth's old man, but as a tragic and undeserved curse.

Generically, it is important to note that the two women writers have produced prose narratives, whereas all three men have written poetry. Is this significant? You may feel that Austen's cool comic irony is closer to the sardonic voice of Percy Shelley than to the impassioned prose of Mary. A comparison of these texts should focus upon the various ways in which each writer has mediated the theme of the Romantic hero and be alert to apparent anomalies such as this.

CHAPTER 5, EXERCISE 2

Comparing Literary Texts: 'The Wife of Bath', *Pride and Prejudice* and 'Anne Hathaway'

The texts, two in poetic form and one in narrative prose, convey particular points of view about the relationships between men and women. The texts portray women at different stages of their lives; the poems present experienced women of the world, both widowed, whereas Elizabeth Bennet is depicted during the courtship period before her marriage to Mr Darcy. Yet all three texts show that assuming that female characters from times past will necessarily reflect the historical inequality between the sexes is overly simplistic. On the contrary, the Wife of Bath's clothing – red stockings, spurs and a hat like a shield or archery target – can be read as symbolic. This 'worthy womman' with her red face, fat bottom and raucous laugh is dressed for battle and fighting the sex war – 'the old daunce'. Her boastful, loud, gossipy nature is presented as exhausting but hugely entertaining, with the narrator apparently taking her word for it that she is the world's greatest weaver and an expert in all affairs of the heart. Her knowledge of 'wandringe by the weye' points to her avoidance of the straight and narrow paths trod by more strait-laced Canterbury pilgrims. The narrative voice of Geoffrey Chaucer is satisfyingly complex. As well as being the poet and architect of the whole *Canterbury Tales* sequence, Chaucer also inserts himself into the text, as a rather too easily impressed pilgrim. This opens up a gap between the all-seeing, narrative puppet-master and the apparently naïve fellow traveller – Chaucer the Poet and Chaucer the Pilgrim. The colloquial voice of the narrator is created partly through a series of chatty passing remarks addressed directly to the reader – 'and that was scathe', 'soothly for to seye', 'I dorste swere'.

It is interesting to see that five marriages have left the Wife of Bath a wealthy, independent woman able to finance adventurous foreign holidays and beholden to no man. The dominant reading position in Chaucer's time may well have condemned this rebellious woman, but a feminist, oppositional reading position will celebrate the Wife's chutzpah and confidence. Conversely, when Jane Austen's Elizabeth Bennet marries Mr Darcy, her identity will change forever and the personal authority and choice she is able to exert before her wedding – shown in her refusal to marry an extremely socially and economically powerful man – may be seen to end when she finally says 'I do'. Perhaps that is why Jane Austen's novels are all about love and romance in the courtship period, where instability and uncertainty prevail. Once married, perhaps women's stories become subsumed into their husbands' – especially if, like Anne Hathaway's, he is a man of immense prestige, fame and significance.

As the wife of William Shakespeare, Anne Hathaway has left little trace upon history. Unlike her husband, no writing by her survives (if, in fact, she could write at all). In her poem, Carol Ann Duffy revoices a traditionally silenced woman using the form of a **dramatic monologue**. This shifting of narrative focus away from Shakespeare's words, publicly enshrined and preserved for all time, and towards his unknown wife provides an alternative feminist point of view.

The poem is from a collection called *The World's Wife*, in which Duffy reclaims several marginalised and stereotyped women. In this sense, 'Anne Hathaway' is part of a larger text, just as the description of the Wife of Bath is part of *The Canterbury Tales* as a whole and the 'General Prologue' in particular. The text involves a clear reversal of expectations in that the will Duffy includes within her text has generally been seen as a sign of Shakespeare's lack of respect and affection for his wife. Duffy's use of the sonnet form is an ironic reflection of its subject matter, because Shakespeare is so closely associated with some of the most famous and beautiful sonnets ever written. Sonnets were traditionally love poems written by men to women; 'Anne Hathaway' reverses this position.

CHAPTER 5, EXERCISE 3

Comparing Non-Literary Texts: Texts A–E

Texts A–E might all be categorised as informative texts about the formation of human relationships – but their audiences, purposes and contexts are clearly very different. Text A is apparently an example of **phatic talk** between two people who know each other very well – a mother and daughter. Yet the pragmatics of the transcript suggests subtle underlying power plays as Jane and Lydia negotiate their conversational agendas. In Jane's terms, the significant events of a day at school are likely to be educational – she is a teacher, after all – but Lydia's priorities are social, to do with being asked out by John, rather than her French test result. Jane's agenda may be initially to check up on her daughter's academic progress, but this is partly disguised by the reference to Abby, apparently one of Lydia's school friends who has been ill. Lydia is not prepared to discuss the French test, however, because her agenda is the complex social ramifications of going out with John, and she becomes exasperated by Jane's persistent digressions from the central conversational topic – as shown by her rising intonation and her use of '*anyway*' – the discourse marker of a major **topic shift** back to her key agenda.

An increasing number of **non-fluency features**, for example repetitions and filler phrases such as 'sort of' and 'you know', may indicate Lydia is slightly uncomfortable with the topic. Interestingly, when Jane realises the real significance of the John episode, her language becomes very supportive, and she encourages Lydia to talk by using prompts such as 'because' followed by a pause indicating that she is waiting for a reply. She tries to facilitate Lydia's choices and decisions, using the modal verb 'might' and lexis such as 'maybe' and offers clear support, 'I think he must just like you'. Ultimately, the conversation is co-operative and mutually supportive, after a rather shaky start.

Unlike Text A, Text B is an example of public rather than private discourse. It targets a specific audience – A Level Communication Studies students keen to develop their knowledge and understanding of a key area of study. The opening paragraph introduces the reader to the subject of group dynamics by addressing them personally, and the use of the personal pronouns 'you', 'we' and 'us' draws the reader in before the discourse becomes more impersonal and the expected formal register of an informative text is established. Lots of declarative statements offer a clear outline of the subject, and **graphological** features, such as the use of a bold font, provide markers of the developing logical argument. The notion of an educated target audience is implicit in the use of sophisticated rhetorical devices such as balanced two-part sentences which encompass an oppositional idea: 'Some are small (say, five people), others are large (say, several hundred).' The text is tightly cohesive, being concerned solely with the topic of groups and concluding with a memorable classification and definition.

Like Text B, Text C is also concerned with investigating the complexities of group decisions and interactions. On the surface, it is a light and entertaining commentary on the process of writing a hugely popular and successful fictional text about 'the differences between men and women'. The text's central conceit compares collaborative screenwriting to two other shared activities – making a pizza and forming a romantic relationship. (Of course, this characteristic linking of food and love also underpinned Ephron's key lime pie recipe, which featured in Chapter 1 of this book.) A **semantic field** of love is suggested from the start when the director claims to be willing to 'commit to' the pizza, although the use of this disproportionately serious phrase actually reinforces the text's light and witty voice. On the other hand, below the colloquial, chatty, humorous style there may lurk a hint of regret. Each proposed addition to the original perfect pizza meets with a more negative come back, until the controversial suggestion of anchovies is not even dignified with a response in direct speech, implying a major disagreement. This progressive disenchantment (traceable in the punctuation of direct speech alone) deftly parallels the gradual cooling of a romantic relationship, and the writer thereby implies that life and love are as irrational, idiosyncratic and fundamentally inconsequential as toppings on a pizza. Ephron also draws attention to the ironic mismatch between fiction and real life by mocking the folly of those who question her about gender roles and romance, as if writing a successful romantic comedy somehow makes her an expert on human relationships.

Since Text D is a parody, its primary purpose is to entertain despite its superficial informative slant. The article's layout supports an informative classification, using bullet points and impersonal imperative sentences giving direct advice such as 'Be a little gay'. Presumably the writer is well aware of the contemporary use of the word 'gay' to mean homosexual, so by using it apparently in its original 1950s sense of 'happy', another layer of humour is added to the text. Each nugget of advice is accompanied by an illustrated example which directly addresses the reader and the final punch line – 'a good wife always knows her place' – is similar in structure to Text B's categorical final statement – 'If there is no interaction between the individuals then a group cannot be formed.'

The pragmatics of Text D suggests that its sophisticated target audience will grasp the grotesque politically incorrect sexism of the piece and get the joke. In fact the message board responses (Text E) show that readers have responded to the text in a variety of ways. The punctuation and spelling errors in several of the responses suggest that taking part in an ongoing web discussion is a form of writing with several of the typical features of speech. Like the conversation in Text A, the responses seem unplanned, spontaneous and casual. Mari defends the sexual roles put forward in *The Good Wife's Guide* while acknowledging that she may be seen as out of step with modern times. Her references to the Bible suggests that she is trying to endorse an unfashionable position by pointing out that God is on her side. Other writers seem angry (Glenn), amused (Joe) and comical (Innocent Bystander – who uses a name obviously designed to conceal his or her identity). Two terse comments even seem to express annoyance at anyone who takes text D too seriously; 'Hoax,' says Daniel; 'it's satire, people,' observes Ary.

One final point of interest is the extent to which intertextual links involve not just Texts A–E themselves, but also some of the literary extracts printed earlier in this chapter. Modern men and women are sometimes presented as not so very far removed from the behaviour and attitudes of the apparently comically old-fashioned 1950s, and still very much caught up in the Wife of Bath's 'old daunce' of sexual politics and sexual attraction. The pragmatics of Texts A and B suggest that modern courtship codes are as elaborate as those of Jane Austen's time, as Lydia is worried about dating a boy who has just been seeing one of her friends, while Nora Ephron offers a bittersweet critique of the acknowledged 'expert' on love and romance all too aware of her own ignorance. Above all, each text has something to say about the central importance to our lives of our relationships with others.

GLOSSARY

Allusion When one text makes a reference to another

Alter ego Literally 'second self'. In literary fiction, an alter ego can be a secondary character who sheds light on a main character when they are compared, or another (usually dark and hidden) side of the main character. Edward Hyde is the alter ego of William Jekyll in the story by R.L. Stevenson

Archetype A perfect or typical example of something. Mr Darcy in *Pride and Prejudice* can be seen as the archetypal romantic hero

Bildungsroman A German term referring to novels about the process of growing up and learning about the world

Byronic hero A character associated with the life and work of George Gordon, Lord Byron – typically a wandering, passionate rebel or outcast

Canon As used in this book, a list of literary texts considered to be unchallengeably great and exceptional works of art

Conceit An exaggerated and far-fetched comparison or metaphor. In the poem 'Valentine', Carol Ann Duffy uses an onion to represent the idea of love

Context Literally 'with the text'. Context looks at the circumstances that affect the production of the text by an author and the circumstances that affect the reception of the text by readers

Cultural capital A term that describes someone's stake in society; the extent to which they feel able to participate in the cultural life of the community in which they live

Demotic Suggesting language spoken by ordinary people

Discourse A continuous piece of written or spoken text, but as used in this book it refers to more than this. Here it refers to the way texts cohere and the ways in which readers recognise this

Dominant reading position   When reading a text we may work out that the author prefers one particular interpretation to others. This is known as the dominant reading position (see also **oppositional reading position**)

Dramatic monologue   A text (usually a poem) in which the writer adopts the **persona** of a speaker or character, for example 'Anne Hathaway' by Carol Ann Duffy

Ephemeral text   A text soon discarded or forgotten

Epistolary novel   A form of text written as a sequence of letters, diary entries or a combination of the two

Enlightenment   A term referring to the widespread European scientific and philosophical movement (*c.* 1700–70) that aimed to replace shallow superstition and bigoted ignorance with religious tolerance and rational understanding

Epic   As used in this book, to a text which recounts events of huge significance (see also **mock epic**)

Genre and subgenre   Genre refers to an identifiable text type. It can be used in a number of ways: to identify a type of writing as in a report, a letter, a poem; and it can identify a group of texts that have subject matter in common as in crime fiction, travel writing, sports writing. Subgenre is a branch of genre, so if the genre is crime fiction, then police procedural is a subgenre

Gothic   This term refers to texts that deal with dramatic supernatural themes, often set in isolated and gloomy locations, such as ruined castles, and featuring episodes of horror, terror and persecution. The most famous Gothic novel in English is Mary Shelley's *Frankenstein*; Jane Austen spoofed the genre in *Northanger Abbey*

Graphology   Aspects of the visual appearance of a text (such as illustrations, fonts, columns and emboldening) that can affect the ways in which it is read and understood

Hyperbole   Deliberately overstated exaggeration for effect – 'hype'

Icon   In this book, a person of great fame and influence who comes to represent a movement, style, time or place

Intertextuality   This refers to the ways in which one text carries echoes or references to other texts

Irony   This is a complex term, but essentially it involves the difference between what is said and what is meant

Lexis   The words in a text

Liminal   In this book, a term used to describe a threshold person living on the margins of society. Often seen as a threat by more conventional members of a group or class

Mock epic   Where epic refers to texts recounting events of huge significance, mock epic takes trivial events and makes them even more trivial by pretending they are of epic proportions

Motif   A recurring pattern or image in a text that may be associated with a particular theme or character

Narrative structure   A narrative is a story, so this term refers to the way the telling of the story is organised

Narrative persona   The persona is the invented voice that presents a narrative – the 'I' of a narrative, which is not necessarily the voice of the author (e.g. Esther Summerson in *Bleak House*)

Narrative voice   The narrative voice is the voice that 'tells' a story. A simple distinction of narrative voice is between **third person** (he/she/they) and **first person** (I) although within these broad categories there are many subtle distinctions

Narrator, narratee   The narrator is the person in a text who appears to be addressing the reader. Narrators can be **omniscient**, **unreliable**, etc. (see below). The narratee is the implied reader of a text, whose identity is built up by a series of assumptions about that reader

Non-fluency features   These are the pauses, repetitions and hesitations that occur naturally as we speak

Objective correlative   A literary term coined by the poet and critic T.S. Eliot in which objects, situations or events are used to represent characters or emotions

Omniscient narrator   The person telling the story who is not part of the action, but knows everything there is to know about it

Oppositional reading position   Although we may recognise a **dominant reading position** (see above), we may nonetheless still wish to take a different view of the text, in which case we take an oppositional reading position

Paradox A statement that seems to contradict itself or defy commonsense

Parody A text which mimics an existing **source** text, drawing attention to key features of its theme, form, language and/or structure for comic effect

Phatic talk Often referred to as 'small talk', phatic talk oils the machinery of social contact and eases speakers into conversations – e.g. 'How are you?'

Polemic A powerful text that argues a strongly controversial case

Pragmatics The way meanings in texts, written or spoken, can work beyond the apparent surface meaning

Register The level of formality of a written or spoken text, dependent on topic, audience, purpose and context

Romanticism This term refers to the artistic and cultural movement that followed on from (and partly reacted against) the **Enlightenment** (see above). The Romantics prioritised originality, imagination and freedom rather than reason, self-restraint and order

Rule of three This term refers to the trick of grouping three things together in a written or spoken text to heighten their impact. Jane Austen used this technique frequently; so did Tony Blair when he claimed his government's priorities were 'Education, education and education'

Satire The use of humour to criticise human behaviour

Semantics and semantic field Semantics is the study of linguistic meaning. A semantic field is a group of words related in meaning as a result of being connected with a particular context of use. 'Shot', 'header', 'tackle' and 'throw-in' are all connected with the semantic field of football

Soliloquy From the Latin for 'solo speaker', this term refers to a speech in which a character alone on stage states his or her thoughts aloud for the benefit of the audience. Conventionally, soliloquies reveal a character's true feelings, with the result that the audience gains inside knowledge unavailable to other characters in the play

Source The original material used and adapted by an author in creating a new text. *Pride and Prejudice* was Helen Fielding's source for *Bridget Jones's Diary*

Subtext The possible hidden meaning(s) below the surface of a text

Topic shift or **topic change** The moment in a conversation when one speaker redirects the focus of the talk to change the subject

Unreliable narrator   The reader cannot trust the person telling the story because they may distort, omit, misrepresent or rearrange the events they are reporting

Vernacular   The ordinary language or dialect of a particular group of people or place

Zeitgeist   A German term meaning 'spirit of the times', often applied to literary texts that seem to sum up the essence of the age or culture that produced them. These are texts with a finger-on-the-pulse feel